MICHIGAN

BUCKET LIST

ADVENTURE

DISCOVER 100 MUST-SEE DESTINATIONS TO CREATE
LASTING MEMORIES AND EXPERIENCE THE BEST OF
THE GREAT LAKES STATE

Disclaimer Notice

The content in this book is for informational and entertainment purposes only. While every effort has been made to ensure the accuracy and completeness of the information contained within, the author and publisher make no representations or warranties regarding the accuracy, applicability, or fitness of the content. The reader assumes full responsibility for their actions, and the author shall not be held liable for any damages, losses, or other consequences arising from the use or misuse of the information provided. This book is not intended to replace professional advice. Consult a licensed professional before attempting any activities or techniques described within.

By purchasing and reading this book, you agree that the author is not responsible for any adverse effects or losses resulting from the application of the information provided.

CONTENT

Iconic & Unique Attractions 71

Scenic Drives & Trails 89

Welcome to Michigan: Your Gateway to Adventure

Welcome to Michigan, a state rich with diversity and adventure, where the landscapes are as varied as the stories they tell. Known as the Great Lakes State, Michigan offers over 3,000 miles of shoreline, dense forests, charming small towns, and lively urban centers. It's a place for explorers, nature lovers, and those who seek to immerse themselves in both breathtaking scenery and vibrant local culture. From the shores of Lake Michigan and the forests of the Upper Peninsula to the art-filled streets of Detroit and Ann Arbor, every corner of Michigan has something unique to offer.

This book is your invitation to discover Michigan's many faces. Think of it as a gateway to both the familiar and the hidden gems of this incredible state, helping you map out adventures that match your travel style. Whether you're an avid hiker, a family traveler, a solo adventurer, or simply someone looking to relax by the water, *Michigan Bucket List Adventure* is here to guide you.

You're about to explore a collection of 100 must-see destinations, covering everything from natural wonders to cultural landmarks. With so much to see, this guide will help you plan, navigate, and make the most of each experience—creating memories that will stay with you long after you leave.

Why a Bucket List Adventure?

A bucket list is more than just a to-do list; it's a map to the experiences that make life rich and fulfilling. In a place like Michigan, where the possibilities for exploration are endless, a bucket list is a perfect way to capture the essence of adventure. This state is home to places that capture the spirit of wonder—be it the quiet stillness of a forest in winter, the roar of waterfalls in the Upper Peninsula, or the lively chatter of beachgoers along Lake Michigan's shores in summer. Michigan's landscapes inspire travelers to embrace new experiences, each offering its own mix of beauty, excitement, and tranquility.

Michigan Bucket List Adventure was created to be a bridge between inspiration and action. It's not just a list of places; it's a carefully curated selection of destinations that represent the best of Michigan's outdoors, cities, and cultural history. Each destination is an opportunity to explore something unique, to try something new, or to revisit a beloved spot with fresh eyes. And because Michigan has such diverse regions, this book allows you to choose the kind of journey you want—whether that's an outdoor escape in the wilderness, a relaxing beach day, or an exploration of the arts and history.

This book is more than a guide; it's a companion to help you connect deeply with Michigan. In these pages, you'll find suggestions that suit a variety of interests, allowing you to shape your own adventure.

Michigan's Seasons and Best Times to Visit ✈

One of the most captivating aspects of Michigan is its distinctly varied seasons, each bringing a unique way to experience the state's landscapes, activities, and atmosphere. Whether you're drawn to the warmth of summer, the vivid colors of autumn, the quiet beauty of winter, or the freshness of spring, Michigan is a destination that offers something special throughout the year. Here's a guide to what each season holds and why it's worth exploring all year round.

Spring (March to May)

Spring in Michigan marks a time of renewal as temperatures gradually rise and nature reawakens. As the snow melts, the landscape comes alive with blooming wildflowers, budding trees, and increased wildlife activity. Spring is ideal for travelers looking to enjoy Michigan's parks and trails in quieter surroundings before the summer crowds arrive. This season also brings festivals and community events that celebrate Michigan's heritage, creating a vibrant atmosphere in towns and cities across the state.

Summer (June to August)

Summer is peak season in Michigan, with warm days and cool evenings providing ideal conditions for outdoor activities. This season is perfect for enjoying the state's extensive coastline, where miles of sandy beaches, crystal-clear waters, and scenic lake views create a lively yet relaxing escape. Summer in Michigan is all about being outdoors—swimming, kayaking, hiking, and exploring the countless natural spaces. Towns across the state come alive with open-air markets, community festivals, and seasonal eateries, making it a dynamic season for anyone seeking an energetic and family-friendly getaway.

Fall (September to November)

Michigan's fall season is a feast for the senses, as vibrant colors transform the landscape into a rich tapestry of red, orange, and gold. Crisp, cool air invites travelers to embark on scenic drives, take leisurely hikes, and enjoy seasonal harvest events. Farms and orchards across the state welcome visitors with apple picking, cider tasting, and other harvest-themed activities. This is also a prime time for winery visits, as the backdrop of autumnal colors enhances the beauty of Michigan's vineyard landscapes. Fall is an ideal season for photographers, families, and anyone looking to immerse themselves in Michigan's peaceful, colorful surroundings.

Winter (December to February)

Winter in Michigan is a true wonderland, creating a haven for snow lovers and winter sports enthusiasts. With significant snowfall in many parts of the state, Michigan is a perfect setting for activities like skiing, snowboarding, snowshoeing, and ice fishing. Trails, parks, and frozen lakes offer a tranquil beauty unique to winter, and many areas embrace the season with cozy lodges, holiday events, and local traditions. Winter in Michigan captures a different side of the state, offering a quiet and reflective experience while inviting travelers to embrace the snow-covered landscapes and festive spirit.

Insider Travel Tips for Michigan

As you set off to explore Michigan's diverse landscapes and vibrant communities, a bit of planning and preparation can go a long way in enhancing your experience. From navigating the open roads to packing for unpredictable weather, these insider tips will help you make the most of your Michigan adventure.

Best Times to Visit

Michigan's peak travel seasons are late spring, summer, and early fall. These months bring ideal weather for outdoor activities, scenic drives, and festival-hopping. If you're planning to enjoy Michigan's beaches and water activities, summer offers warm temperatures and long daylight hours. Fall, with its stunning foliage and crisp air, is perfect for those who enjoy scenic views and quieter, reflective getaways. Winter is also a special time for those who appreciate snow sports and holiday festivities, though it requires an extra layer of preparation for cold conditions.

Transportation and Getting Around

To fully experience Michigan's array of destinations and landscapes, renting a car is often the best option. Having a vehicle allows for flexibility, letting you explore both popular attractions and lesser-known areas at your own pace. Michigan's extensive road network makes driving straightforward, and a car is particularly useful for reaching remote natural areas. For island visits or more isolated destinations, ferries and seasonal transport options are available.

Packing Essentials

Michigan's weather can change quickly, so packing layers is essential. Even in summer, temperatures can dip in the evenings, especially near the water or in forested areas. Comfortable, sturdy shoes are a must, as you'll likely be doing a lot of walking, whether you're exploring city streets, sandy beaches, or forest trails. A camera is always recommended— Michigan's diverse landscapes provide countless photo opportunities, from sunrise over the Great Lakes to autumnal forests and snowy winter scenes. Other essentials include sunscreen for sunny days, bug spray for forested or lakeside areas, and a reusable water bottle to stay hydrated.

Accommodation Tips

Michigan offers a range of accommodation options, from rustic cabins and cozy bed-and-breakfasts to lakeside resorts and modern hotels. During peak seasons, especially in popular areas, it's best to book accommodations in advance to secure your preferred options. For a unique experience, consider staying in a local inn or lodge, where you can enjoy a more personal connection with Michigan's communities. Many regions also offer campgrounds for those who enjoy camping, adding an extra element of adventure to your stay.

Respecting Nature and Local Spaces

Michigan's natural beauty is one of its greatest assets, and preserving it requires responsible travel practices. When exploring parks, trails, and beaches, be mindful of leave-no-trace principles: pack out all waste, stay on designated paths, and avoid disturbing wildlife. Respect for local communities is also key. Many small towns and rural areas in Michigan are proud of their heritage and environment, so being considerate of local customs and spaces enhances the experience for both travelers and residents alike.

Seasonal Considerations

Each season in Michigan requires a slightly different approach to travel:

- Spring and Fall: Pack layers and prepare for cooler temperatures, especially in the mornings and evenings. Be aware of seasonal allergies, as spring brings pollen and fall has leaf mold.
- Summer: Summer can be humid, so pack breathable fabrics, sun protection, and plenty of water. Remember, even on hot days, lake temperatures can be cool.
- Winter: For winter visits, dress in warm layers and pack waterproof boots, gloves, hats, and scarves. Plan for extra travel time if driving, as snowy and icy conditions are common.

Navigating Michigan's Geography

Michigan's geography is as unique as it is expansive, offering travelers a mix of urban hubs, scenic coastlines, dense forests, and tranquil rural areas. The state is divided into two major landmasses—the Lower Peninsula and the Upper Peninsula—each with its own character and attractions. Familiarizing yourself with Michigan's layout will help you plan a journey that flows seamlessly from one experience to the next, making the most of each region's distinct qualities.

The Lower Peninsula

The Lower Peninsula, often referred to as "the Mitten" due to its shape, is Michigan's most populous and developed region. Here, you'll find a blend of bustling cities, picturesque small towns, and popular lakefront areas. This part of Michigan is known for its accessibility and variety. The western coast of the Lower Peninsula is home to miles of sandy beaches along Lake Michigan, drawing beachgoers, families, and outdoor enthusiasts, especially in the warmer months.

Meanwhile, the eastern side, bordered by Lake Huron, offers a quieter, more rural experience, ideal for travelers looking to escape the crowds. The Lower Peninsula also hosts Michigan's largest cities, including Detroit and Grand Rapids, which feature rich histories, vibrant arts scenes, and a wide array of dining, shopping, and entertainment options. This region's varied attractions make it a flexible choice for all kinds of travelers, from city explorers to beach lovers.

The Upper Peninsula

The Upper Peninsula, or "the U.P." as locals call it, is renowned for its rugged beauty and more secluded atmosphere. Bordered by Lake Superior to the north and Lake Michigan to the south, the Upper Peninsula is an outdoor paradise, with vast forests, rocky shores, and peaceful trails. This region is less populated than the Lower Peninsula, offering a more remote and wilderness-focused experience.

The U.P. is ideal for travelers looking for a slower pace, where they can immerse themselves in nature and escape the fast pace of everyday life. The climate in the U.P. tends to be cooler than in the Lower Peninsula, making it a perfect summer retreat for those who enjoy hiking, camping, and exploring off-the-beaten-path destinations. During winter, this area becomes a haven for snow sports, with abundant snowfall and trails for skiing, snowmobiling, and snowshoeing. The Upper Peninsula is cherished for its natural beauty, friendly communities, and close-knit feel, making it a rewarding destination for travelers seeking authentic experiences.

Understanding Distances and Travel Times

Michigan's layout is deceptively large, and while many of its highlights are reachable within a day's drive, it's worth planning with travel times in mind. The Lower Peninsula's attractions are generally more accessible, with well-connected highways and shorter distances between cities and towns. However, if you're venturing into the Upper Peninsula, keep in mind that some areas are more remote, and travel times can be longer due to the region's expansive, rugged terrain.

To cross between the two peninsulas, travelers can take the scenic Mackinac Bridge, one of the longest suspension bridges in the world, connecting the Lower and Upper Peninsulas. For those exploring the Lake Michigan coast, there are also ferry services that operate seasonally, allowing you to reach certain points along the shoreline or island destinations.

Exploring by Region

Michigan's layout lends itself well to regional exploration. Many travelers find it helpful to divide their visit by region, focusing on one area at a time to fully experience its unique offerings. Popular approaches include:

- Exploring the Lake Michigan Coastline: Following the shoreline of Lake Michigan, visitors can discover beach towns, dunes, and scenic byways, making for a relaxed and picturesque journey.
- Discovering the Inland Lakes and Forests: Central Michigan is filled with inland lakes and woodlands, ideal for nature lovers seeking peace and tranquility.
- Urban Exploration in Major Cities: From the historic heart of Detroit to the artistic vibes of Ann Arbor and the craft breweries of Grand Rapids, Michigan's cities each have their own character and are best enjoyed through immersive exploration.

Michigan's diverse geography is part of what makes it such an exciting destination. Whether you're drawn to the beach, the woods, or the city lights, this state has an array of landscapes that invite you to explore every corner.

Michigan's Outdoor Etiquette and Conservation

Michigan's natural beauty is one of its most cherished qualities, attracting travelers who come to experience the pristine beaches, dense forests, and abundant wildlife. With such a wealth of outdoor spaces to enjoy, it's essential to practice responsible travel habits that help protect these environments for future generations. By following a few simple guidelines, you can contribute to the preservation of Michigan's natural wonders while ensuring that your experience remains respectful and rewarding.

Respect the Leave-No-Trace Principles

Whether you're hiking a trail, enjoying a beach day, or camping in one of Michigan's parks, following leave-no-trace principles is a fundamental way to minimize your impact on the environment. These principles include:

- Packing Out Waste: Take all trash, food scraps, and personal items with you when you leave. Michigan's parks and trails often provide waste bins, but it's always best to come prepared to carry out any waste, especially in more remote areas.
- Staying on Marked Trails: Michigan's trails and pathways are designed to protect both visitors and the surrounding environment. Staying on designated paths helps prevent erosion, protects native plants, and reduces the risk of getting lost.
- Respecting Wildlife: Michigan is home to diverse wildlife, from deer and foxes to various bird species. Observe animals from a distance, avoid feeding them, and do not disturb their natural habitats.

Be Mindful of Fire Safety

Many travelers enjoy campfires as part of the Michigan outdoor experience, especially during camping trips. However, fire safety is crucial in protecting Michigan's forests and natural areas. Before starting a fire, always check local regulations, as certain areas may have restrictions or bans during dry seasons. Use designated fire rings where available, keep fires small, and never leave them unattended. Fully extinguish all fires before leaving a campsite to prevent accidental wildfires.

Water Conservation and Lake Respect

Michigan's many lakes, rivers, and streams are central to its outdoor appeal. When enjoying these water sources, be mindful of your impact. Avoid using soaps or other chemicals in natural water sources, as even biodegradable products can disrupt aquatic ecosystems. If you're kayaking, fishing, or boating, follow local guidelines to ensure that you're protecting Michigan's lakes and rivers, especially in sensitive areas where invasive species may be a concern.

Supporting Conservation Efforts

Michigan has a robust network of conservation programs aimed at preserving its unique ecosystems. Consider supporting local conservation efforts by visiting state parks and paying entrance fees, which often fund environmental protection initiatives. Many parks also offer volunteer programs where travelers can participate in clean-up days, trail maintenance, or wildlife monitoring. These programs are a great way to give back to the places you're exploring and to learn more about Michigan's environmental efforts.

Respect Local Communities and Their Spaces

Many of Michigan's most beautiful destinations are in or near small towns and communities that value their natural surroundings. Being considerate of local residents—whether by adhering to noise ordinances, parking responsibly, or supporting local businesses—helps maintain a positive relationship between travelers and residents. Engaging with local culture by respecting traditions, supporting local artisans, or even just greeting locals warmly enriches your travel experience and fosters a sense of connection to the area.

Eco-Friendly Travel Choices

When exploring Michigan, consider ways to make your travel more eco-friendly. Bringing reusable items such as water bottles, bags, and food containers helps reduce single-use waste. Additionally, using public transportation, carpooling, or biking when possible are great ways to lessen your environmental footprint. Small choices, like choosing local products over imported goods or visiting eco-conscious businesses, add up and support Michigan's efforts to create sustainable, environmentally-friendly tourism.

Michigan's natural beauty is both a gift and a responsibility, and each visitor plays a role in preserving it. By embracing these outdoor etiquette practices, you're not only protecting the environment but also helping to ensure that Michigan remains a place of wonder and inspiration for years to come.

Using This Guide for a Personalized Experience

Michigan Bucket List Adventure is designed to be more than just a travel guide; it's a resource that allows you to tailor each adventure to your unique interests and style. With over 100 carefully selected destinations spanning Michigan's landscapes, history, and culture, this guide invites you to explore the state at your own pace, uncovering both iconic sites and hidden gems. Here's how to make the most of this book on your journey.

Building Your Own Bucket List

This guide offers a diverse selection of destinations, giving you the freedom to pick and choose the experiences that resonate with you. As you go through the book, you might find places that instantly capture your interest or locations you want to revisit during a different season. Use this guide to create a Michigan bucket list that reflects your personal travel goals, whether they include relaxing beach days, adventurous hikes, cultural discoveries, or family-friendly outings.

Adapting to Different Travel Styles

This book is crafted to appeal to a variety of travel styles. Whether you're a solo explorer, a family traveler, or a couple seeking a romantic getaway, you'll find destinations and experiences that suit your preferences. Adventure seekers will discover rugged trails and challenging climbs, while those who prefer a slower pace will appreciate the scenic drives, serene lakes, and welcoming small towns. Each section of the book is designed with flexibility in mind, allowing you to shape your trip to fit your interests.

Space for Reflection and Personal Notes

This guide is not just a list of destinations but a keepsake for your journey. In addition to exploring Michigan's landscapes, you'll find dedicated spaces within the book to jot down notes, reflections, and memorable moments from each destination. Use these sections to document your thoughts, write about special experiences, and even add ideas for future visits. By the end of your travels, you'll have a personalized record of your Michigan adventures that you can look back on for years to come.

Seasonal Suggestions and Flexible Planning

Michigan's seasonal variety means that each destination offers a unique experience depending on the time of year. As you plan your itinerary, consider how different seasons may enhance or change your visit. From summer's beach vibes to winter's snowy serenity, each season brings new perspectives to Michigan's natural and cultural sites. The guide's flexible structure allows you to plan around seasonal highlights, ensuring that you get the most out of every trip, no matter when you go.

Capturing Memories and Inspiring Future Adventures

Each destination in this guide is a starting point for memories, but they're also invitations to discover more. As you explore Michigan, you may be inspired to return to favorite spots or discover new places nearby. This book is designed to be a companion that grows with your experiences, encouraging you to keep expanding your Michigan bucket list. Use it as a tool not only to plan trips but to inspire future journeys, creating a lasting connection to the state.

Enhance Your Adventure with LocalListingX

Welcome to *LocalListingX by Infinite Ink Press*, your essential digital companion for exploring every corner of Michigan! Designed to make your travel planning seamless, this interactive platform is more than just a website—it's a complete guide that adds convenience, detail, and inspiration to each step of your journey.

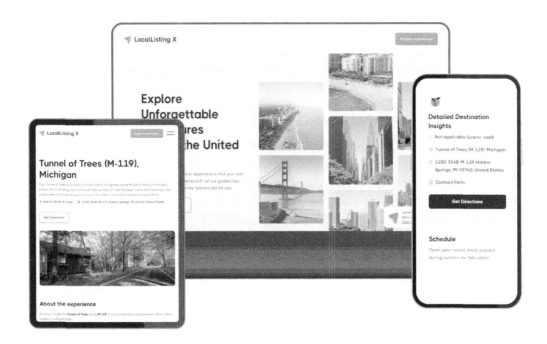

Why LocalListingX is the Perfect Travel Companion

With *LocalListingX*, each destination from the book is enriched with a wealth of information to make your experience smoother and more fulfilling. Here's what you'll find:

- **In-Depth Destination Insights:** Access full details for each location, including contact information, address, ticket links, hours, and direct access to the destination's official website.
- **Interactive Maps:** Each page features dynamic maps that guide you with precise directions from your current location, ensuring you can navigate Michigan's wonders effortlessly.
- **Curated Local Activities:** Discover carefully selected activities through our partnerships with Viator and Get Your Guide. Whether you're seeking outdoor adventures, cultural tours, or family-friendly outings, our platform connects you to the best experiences nearby.
- **Vivid Imagery:** Preview each destination with beautiful photos that capture the essence of Michigan's landscapes and attractions, helping you plan a memorable visit.

Single Destination Pages

Each destination has a dedicated page on *LocalListingX*, where you'll find everything you need to explore confidently. These pages include essential info such as directions, hours, ticketing options, and related activities. Whether you're preparing for a quick stop or planning a day trip, these pages give you all the details to make the most of your visit.

Activities and Related Experiences

Our platform goes beyond destination details by linking each location to nearby activities from trusted providers like Viator and Get Your Guide. From thrilling outdoor adventures to insightful guided tours, *LocalListingX* makes it easy to find activities that match your interests. Each recommendation is vetted, allowing you to confidently explore everything Michigan has to offer.

Easy Navigation for Seamless Travel

To make exploration as smooth as possible, *LocalListingX* includes:

- Search Bar: Looking for something specific? Use our intuitive search bar to find destinations, activities, or categories quickly.
- Sort by Category: Whether you're interested in nature parks, historical sites, or unique attractions, our platform organizes destinations by category, making it easy to explore what Michigan offers based on your interests.
- Downloadable Map: For a complete overview, access our downloadable map with all destinations and activities in one place—perfect for trip planning or offline use.

How LocalListingX Complements Your Guide

While the book provides a curated list of Michigan's top destinations, *LocalListingX* takes your journey further. Use it to access up-to-date contact information, directions, and personalized activity suggestions—all from your mobile device. Whether you're at home planning or on the road exploring, this platform ensures you have everything you need right at your fingertips.

How to Use LocalListingX with This Book

Each destination in the book features a QR code. Simply scan the QR code with your phone to go directly to the destination's page on *LocalListingX*. There, you'll find additional insights and options to enrich your experience.

The *LocalListingX* platform is the ultimate tool for travelers, offering an engaging and interactive way to explore Michigan's best destinations. Visit www.infiniteinkpress.org and start your adventure today!

LocalListing X Website

Downloadable Map

Adventure Awaits! Time to Plan, Pack, and Go!

Are You Ready?

Michigan Map

Download the interactive map by scanning the QR code below.

Travel Destination Checklist

How many can you check off? Think you've got what it takes to visit them all? Or are you already planning which ones you'll "accidentally" skip (we see you, winter hikers!)? Whether you're an all-in adventurer or a selective sightseer, this checklist is here to track your triumphs and keep you motivated.

Natural Wonders & Parks

- O Sleeping Bear Dunes National Lakeshore
- O Pictured Rocks National Lakeshore
- O Tahquamenon Falls State Park
- O Porcupine Mountains Wilderness State Park
- O Isle Royale National Park
- O Mackinac Island State Park
- O Silver Lake Sand Dunes
- O Warren Dunes State Park
- O Ludington State Park
- O Palms Book State Park (Kitch-iti-kipi)
- O Ocqueoc Falls
- O Bond Falls
- O Lake of the Clouds
- O Keweenaw Peninsula
- O Leelanau State Park

Historical & Cultural Sites

- O The Village at Grand Traverse Commons
- O Colonial Michilimackinac
- O Mackinac Island Historical Museum
- O Zekelman Holocaust Center
- O The Gilmore Car Museum
- O Greenfield Village
- O Fort Mackinac
- O The Ford Piquette Avenue Plant Museum
- O The Detroit Institute of Arts (DIA)
- O Motown Museum
- O Gerald R. Ford Presidential Museum
- O Frederik Meijer Gardens & Sculpture Park
- O Castle Farms
- O The Guardian Building

Iconic & Unique Attractions

- O Mackinac Bridge
- O Comerica Park

O The Henry Ford Museum of American Innovation	O Ford Field
O Little Caesars Arena	O Mackinac Island Carriage Tours
O Detroit Zoo, Royal Oak	O Old Mission Peninsula Wine Trail
O Great Lakes Crossing Outlets, Auburn Hills	O North Country Trail (Michigan Section)
O Frankenmuth River Place Shops	O Tahquamenon Falls River Trail, Michigan
O Somerset Collection, Troy	O Iron Belle Trail
O Bronner's CHRISTmas Wonderland	O Turnip Rock Kayak Trail
O The Original Mackinac Island Butterfly House & Insect World	O Iron Ore Heritage Trail
O Air Zoo Aerospace & Science Museum	O Leelanau Peninsula Wine Trail
O Detroit International RiverWalk, Detroit	O Sleeping Bear Heritage Trail
O The Fisher Building	**Beach Destinations**
O The Fisher Building	O Oval Beach
O Detroit People Mover, Detroit	O South Haven Beaches (South Haven Lighthouses)
O The Grand Hotel, Mackinac Island	O Grand Haven State Park
O Belle Isle Aquarium	O Silver Beach County Park
Scenic Drives & Trails	O St. Joseph Lighthouses
O Tunnel of Trees (M-119)	O New Buffalo Public Beach
O Pierce Stocking Scenic Drive	O Lake Michigan Beach Park
O Empire Bluff Trail	O Pere Marquette Park (Muskegon)

O Brockway Mountain Drive	O Ann Arbor Hands-On Museum
O Kal-Haven Trail	O Detroit Historical Museum
O Cheboygan State Park Beach	O Empire Beach
O Belle Isle Beach (Detroit)	O Caseville Beach
O Oscoda Beach Park	O Kensington Metropark
O Manistee North Pierhead Lighthouse	O Michigan Science Center
O Bay City State Park Beach	O Cranbrook Institute of Science
O Sleeping Bear Bay Beach	O LEGOLAND Discovery Center Michigan

Wineries & Breweries

Flint Children's Museum

O Chateau Chantal Winery & Tasting Room	O SEA LIFE Michigan Aquarium
O Brys Estate Vineyard & Winery	O Educational & Museums
O Mari Vineyards	O University of Michigan Museum of Natural History
O Tabor Hill Winery	O Charles H. Wright Museum of African American History
O Round Barn Winery	O Grand Rapids Public Museum
O Founders Brewing Co.	O Cranbrook Art Museum
O St. Julian Winery	O Kalamazoo Institute of Arts

Family-Friendly Attractions

Great Lakes Shipwreck Museum

O John Ball Zoo	Muskegon Museum of Art
O Binder Park Zoo	

Create Your Own Michigan Bucket List

Travel Packing List

Number of Nights:	Weather:	Temperature:
	☀ ⛅ ☁ 🌧 ⛈ 🌨	

QTY			QTY		
		○			○
		○			○
		○			○
		○			○
		○			○
		○			○
		○			○
		○			○
		○			○
		○			○
		○			○
		○			○
		○			○
		○			○
		○			○
		○			○
		○			○
		○			○
		○			○
		○			○
		○			○
		○			○
		○			○
		○			○
		○			○
		○			○
		○			○
		○			○
		○			○

Travel Planner

Destinations	Travel Dates

	Top Things to See and Do

To Do Before Leaving

-
-
-
-
-
-
-
-

Transportation Overview

Depart	Arrive	Date	Time	Type	Carrier#	Booked?

Accommodation Overview

Name	Location	Dates	Type	Address	Contact	Booked?

Travel Packing List

Number of Nights:	Weather:	Temperature:
	☀ ⛅ ☁ 🌧 ⛈ 🌨	

QTY			QTY		
		○			○
		○			○
		○			○
		○			○
		○			○
		○			○
		○			○
		○			○
		○			○
		○			○
		○			○
		○			○
		○			○
		○			○
		○			○
		○			○
		○			○
		○			○
		○			○
		○			○
		○			○
		○			○
		○			○
		○			○
		○			○
		○			○
		○			○
		○			○
		○			○
		○			○

Travel Planner

Destinations	Travel Dates

	Top Things to See and Do

To Do Before Leaving

-
-
-
-
-
-
-
-

Transportation Overview

Depart	Arrive	Date	Time	Type	Carrier#	Booked?

Accommodation Overview

Name	Location	Dates	Type	Address	Contact	Booked?

Travel Packing List

Number of Nights:	Weather:	Temperature:

QTY			QTY		
		○			○
		○			○
		○			○
		○			○
		○			○
		○			○
		○			○
		○			○
		○			○
		○			○
		○			○
		○			○
		○			○
		○			○
		○			○
		○			○
		○			○
		○			○
		○			○
		○			○
		○			○
		○			○
		○			○
		○			○
		○			○
		○			○
		○			○
		○			○
		○			○

Travel Planner

Destinations	Travel Dates

	Top Things to See and Do

To Do Before Leaving

-
-
-
-
-
-
-
-

Transportation Overview

Depart	Arrive	Date	Time	Type	Carrier#	Booked?

Accommodation Overview

Name	Location	Dates	Type	Address	Contact	Booked?

Travel Packing List

Number of Nights:	Weather:	Temperature:
	☀ ⛅ ☁ 🌧 ⛈ 🌨	

QTY			QTY		
		○			○
		○			○
		○			○
		○			○
		○			○
		○			○
		○			○
		○			○
		○			○
		○			○
		○			○
		○			○
		○			○
		○			○
		○			○
		○			○
		○			○
		○			○
		○			○
		○			○
		○			○
		○			○
		○			○
		○			○
		○			○
		○			○
		○			○
		○			○
		○			○
		○			○

Travel Planner

Destinations	Travel Dates

Top Things to See and Do	

To Do Before Leaving

-
-
-
-
-
-
-
-

Transportation Overview

Depart	Arrive	Date	Time	Type	Carrier#	Booked?

Accommodation Overview

Name	Location	Dates	Type	Address	Contact	Booked?

Loading Your Next Travel Adventure!

Are You Ready?

 **LocalListing X**

Welcome to Michigan's 100 Must-See Destinations

We're thrilled to share these incredible places with you and truly hope that each destination brings you as much joy and inspiration as it has brought us. From breathtaking natural wonders to hidden gems and vibrant cultural spots, every place on this list is a unique piece of Michigan's story. Enjoy the journey, and may these experiences create lasting memories!!

Natural Wonders & Parks

Notes

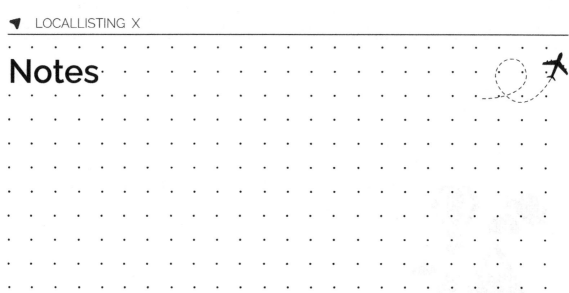

Natural Wonders & Parks | 📍 9922 Front Street, Empire, MI 49630

Sleeping Bear Dunes National Lakeshore

Towering over Lake Michigan's shoreline, Sleeping Bear Dunes National Lakeshore is a stunning blend of dramatic natural beauty and deep cultural roots. The park's iconic dunes rise up to 450 feet above the lake, sculpted by wind and water over millennia. According to Anishinaabe legend, these dunes symbolize a mother bear waiting for her lost cubs, who are remembered as the nearby Manitou Islands. The lakeshore stretches for 35 miles, offering visitors a serene escape filled with picturesque views, peaceful beaches, and lush forests teeming with wildlife. Whether it's hiking the dunes or kayaking in the crystal-clear waters, the park invites exploration and a deep connection to the natural world.

Key Attractions:

- Dune Climb: Adventurers are drawn to the Dune Climb, a challenging ascent that rewards climbers with breathtaking views of Lake Michigan and the surrounding landscape. The expansive dunes provide both a sense of isolation and a unique perspective on the area's geological history.
- Pierce Stocking Scenic Drive: This 7.4-mile loop takes visitors on a journey through dense forest and sandy bluffs, with several scenic overlooks offering panoramic views of the dunes, lake, and surrounding forests. It's a photographer's dream and a must-do for any visitor.
- Manitou Islands: Accessible by ferry, North and South Manitou Islands offer secluded beaches, hiking trails, and opportunities for wilderness camping. These remote islands provide a quiet,

untouched experience, far removed from the crowds of the mainland.

Best Time to Visit:

The ideal visiting months are between May and October, with warm summer days perfect for swimming and hiking, and autumn offering breathtaking foliage.

Operating Hours:

Open year-round. Visitor centers typically operate from 9 AM to 5 PM, with varying hours by season.

Entrance Fees:

- Private Vehicle: $25 (valid for 1-7 days)
- Annual Pass: $45 for unlimited visits in one year

Cashless payments are required at staffed locations; cash is accepted at self-pay stations

Your Digital Travel Companion
Scan to find recommended activities, digital guides, and beautiful images of this place.

🏔 Natural Wonders & Parks | 📍 N8391 Sand Point Road, Munising, MI 49862

Pictured Rocks National Lakeshore

Pictured Rocks National Lakeshore is a breathtaking natural gem located along Lake Superior's southern shoreline in Michigan's Upper Peninsula. The park is known for its towering multicolored sandstone cliffs, tranquil beaches, and inland lakes. Spanning over 42 miles of shoreline, the park offers diverse experiences through hiking, kayaking, and sightseeing, with nearly 100 miles of trails and opportunities to explore natural and historic sites.

Key Attractions

- Cliffs and Rock Formations: The iconic sandstone cliffs rise 50 to 200 feet above Lake Superior, offering spectacular views and geological marvels such as arches and caves.
- Waterfalls: Some of the most notable waterfalls include Munising Falls, Miners Falls, and Sable Falls, easily accessible through short hikes.
- Beaches: Popular beaches include Sand Point Beach and Twelvemile

Beach, perfect for swimming, sunbathing, and picnicking.

Best Time to Visit

Open year-round, Pictured Rocks offers something unique each season: summer is ideal for hiking and water activities, autumn boasts vibrant foliage, winter allows for ice climbing and skiing, and spring brings birdwatching and wildflowers.

Operating Hours

The park is accessible 24/7 all year, though some roads and facilities close in winter. Visitor centers have seasonal hours.

Entrance Fees

- Per Person: $15 for 7 days (on foot, by bike, or boat)
- Private Vehicle: $25 for 7 days
- Motorcycle: $20
- Annual Pass: $45 for unlimited visits (12 months)

Your Digital Travel Companion
Scan to find recommended activities, digital guides, and beautiful images of this place.

Natural Wonders & Parks | 📍 41382 West M-123, Paradise, MI 49768

Tahquamenon Falls State Park

Tahquamenon Falls State Park, located in Michigan's Upper Peninsula, is renowned for its spectacular waterfalls and vast wilderness. The park covers nearly 50,000 acres and stretches across more than 13 miles. The Upper Falls is the crown jewel, a 200-foot-wide, 50-foot-high waterfall, making it one of the largest east of the Mississippi River. The river's unique amber hue, caused by tannins from nearby forests, adds to its beauty. The park is also home to the Lower Falls, a series of smaller cascades.

Key Attractions:

- Upper Falls: The largest and most famous, dropping 50 feet and spanning 200 feet across. Multiple viewing platforms, including a gorge view and brink view, are accessible via well-maintained paths and staircases.
- Lower Falls: A series of five smaller waterfalls surrounding an island. Visitors can explore the falls on foot or rent rowboats for a closer experience.
- River Trail: A popular 4-mile hiking trail connecting the Upper and Lower Falls, offering scenic river views along the way.

Best Time to Visit

The park is open year-round, with each season offering unique experiences. Summer is perfect for hiking and enjoying the falls, while autumn brings stunning foliage. Winter activities include snowshoeing, ice fishing, and viewing frozen waterfalls.

Operating Hours

The park is open 24 hours a day, all year long. However, facilities such as the visitor center and gift shop may have seasonal hours.

Entrance Fees:

- Michigan Residents: $12 for an annual Recreation Passport (for all Michigan state parks).
- Non-Residents: $9 for a day pass or $34 for an annual pass.

Your Digital Travel Companion

Scan to find recommended activities, digital guides, and beautiful images of this place.

Natural Wonders & Parks | 📍 33303 Headquarters Road, Ontonagon, MI 49953

Porcupine Mountains Wilderness State Park

Porcupine Mountains Wilderness State Park, known as "the Porkies," is Michigan's largest state park, covering nearly 60,000 acres of pristine wilderness. Located along the shores of Lake Superior, the park features old-growth forests, dramatic waterfalls, rivers, and rugged terrain that attract outdoor enthusiasts year-round. With over 90 miles of trails and a range of outdoor activities, the Porkies offer an escape into one of the most remote and beautiful areas of the Midwest.

Key Attractions:

- Lake of the Clouds: This famous scenic overlook offers panoramic views of the lake and surrounding wilderness. The viewpoint is ADA-accessible, and the short walk from the parking lot is perfect for all visitors.
- Summit Peak: Standing at nearly 2,000 feet, Summit Peak is the highest point in the park. A short hike leads to an observation tower that provides breathtaking views of the surrounding forest and Lake Superior on clear days.
- Presque Isle River Corridor: Known for its waterfalls and dramatic river views, this area offers several boardwalks and viewing platforms along the Presque Isle River.

Best Time to Visit

The park is open year-round, with each season offering a different experience. Spring and summer are ideal for hiking, fishing, and camping, while autumn showcases stunning fall foliage.

Operating Hours

The park is open 24/7 throughout the year, but the Visitor Center is typically open daily from 8 AM to 6 PM from mid-May through mid-October. During the off-season, it remains closed.

Entrance Fees

- Michigan Residents: $12 for an annual Recreation Passport.
- Non-Residents: $9 for a day pass or $34 for an annual pass

Your Digital Travel Companion
Scan to find recommended activities, digital guides, and beautiful images of this place.

Natural Wonders & Parks | 📍 800 East Lakeshore Drive, Houghton, MI 49931

Isle Royale National Park

Isle Royale National Park is a remote, rugged wilderness located in Lake Superior, Michigan. Known for its isolation and pristine environment, this archipelago consists of over 400 islands, the largest being Isle Royale itself. The park offers a true backcountry experience, with activities like hiking, boating, and scuba diving, as well as opportunities to explore its diverse ecosystems.

Key Attractions:

- Greenstone Ridge Trail: This 40-mile trail is the backbone of Isle Royale, offering stunning views of Lake Superior, inland lakes, and ridges. It's popular for multi-day backpacking trips.
- Lake of the Clouds Overlook: A scenic viewpoint offering panoramic views of this picturesque lake nestled in the park's wilderness.
- Scuba Diving: Explore an underwater museum of shipwrecks, including the famous wreck of "The America."

- Lighthouses: Isle Royale is home to several historic lighthouses, such as Rock Harbor Light and Passage Island Light.

Best Time to Visit

The park is open from April 16 to October 31, after which it closes for the winter due to harsh weather conditions. The best time to visit is late summer (August), when the weather is warm, and bugs are fewer.

Operating Hours

The park is accessible 24 hours a day during the open season, but visitor services such as the Rock Harbor Visitor Center operate during the day, depending on the season.

Entrance Fees:

- Daily Fee: $7 per person per day (children 15 and under are free).
- Season Pass: $60, valid for up to four people from April 16 to October 31. Federal passes are also accepted for up to four individuals

Your Digital Travel Companion

Scan to find recommended activities, digital guides, and beautiful images of this place.

Natural Wonders & Parks | 🅿 Mackinac Island State Park, 7029 Huron Rd, Mackinac Island, MI 49757

Mackinac Island State Park

Mackinac Island State Park, located on Michigan's Mackinac Island, is a beautifully preserved area filled with natural wonders, historic landmarks, and no motor vehicles. Over 80% of the island is covered by the park, making it a haven for cyclists, hikers, and history enthusiasts. Established in 1895, it was Michigan's first state park and previously served as a national park.

Key Attractions:

- Arch Rock: A natural limestone arch rising 146 feet above Lake Huron, offering breathtaking views of the water. It's accessible 24/7 and free to visit.
- Fort Mackinac: A historic military outpost dating back to 1780, offering interactive exhibits and daily reenactments. Admission is around $15 for adults and $9 for children.
- Sugar Loaf: A towering limestone rock formation, one of the island's most impressive natural features.

- British Landing: This scenic area offers peaceful picnic spots and access to biking and hiking trails.

Best Time to Visit

The park is open year-round, but the best time to visit is between May and October when visitor centers and seasonal attractions, such as Fort Mackinac and the Butterfly House, are open.

Operating Hours

The park is open 24 hours a day, all year round. However, visitor centers and facilities such as the Milliken Nature Center and the British Landing Nature Center operate from May through October, typically from 9 AM to 6 PM.

Entrance Fees

There is no general admission fee to explore the park, but historic sites like Fort Mackinac and Mackinac Art Museum have entrance fees. Combination tickets for multiple sites are available for around $30 for adults.

Your Digital Travel Companion

Scan to find recommended activities, digital guides, and beautiful images of this place.

Natural Wonders & Parks | 9679 W, State Park Road, Mears, MI 49436

Silver Lake Sand Dunes

Located on the shores of Lake Michigan, Silver Lake Sand Dunes offers a unique combination of sandy beaches, towering dunes, and off-road adventure. Spanning nearly 2,000 acres, the park allows visitors to explore expansive dunes, scenic landscapes, and enjoy a variety of outdoor activities.

Key Attractions:

- ORV Area: One of the only places in the U.S. where you can drive your own off-road vehicle on sand dunes. The 450-acre ORV area is open from April 1 to October 31 and is a haven for adrenaline seekers looking to test their 4x4s, ATVs, or dune buggies. Visitors can also rent vehicles from local operators like SunBuggy and Silver Lake Buggy Rentals.
- Mac Wood's Dune Rides: Since 1930, Mac Wood's has offered guided 40-minute dune tours, showcasing the unique landscape and history of the dunes. It's perfect for families or those who want to explore the dunes without driving.

Best Time to Visit

The best time to visit Silver Lake Sand Dunes is from May to October, with warmer weather perfect for dune riding, hiking, and water activities. The peak season is during summer, especially on weekends, when the ORV area is most crowded.

Operating Hours

The dunes are open from 9 AM to 8 PM, but hours may vary in early spring and late fall. ORV access requires a parking voucher on weekends and holidays from mid-May through Labor Day, which helps manage the high volume of visitors.

Entrance Fees

A Michigan Recreation Passport ($12 annually for residents or $9 daily for non-residents) is required for entry. For those using the ORV area, an additional ORV license and trail permit are required, which can be purchased at the park's welcome center.

Your Digital Travel Companion

Scan to find recommended activities, digital guides, and beautiful images of this place.

🏔 Natural Wonders & Parks | 📍 12032 Red Arrow Highway, Sawyer, MI 49125

Warren Dunes State Park

Warren Dunes State Park, located in southwest Michigan along Lake Michigan's shoreline, spans 1,952 acres and is known for its massive dunes, beautiful beaches, and extensive recreation opportunities. Tower Hill, the park's tallest dune, rises 240 feet above the lake, offering visitors stunning views and exciting outdoor experiences.

Key Attractions:

- Towering Dunes: The dunes, including Tower Hill, offer thrilling opportunities for hiking, sandboarding, and sledding in the winter.
- Beaches: Warren Dunes features three miles of Lake Michigan shoreline, perfect for swimming, sunbathing, and building sandcastles.
- Hiking Trails: There are six miles of trails through dunes and wooded areas, offering moderate to challenging hikes with scenic views year-round.

Best Time to Visit

The park is open year-round, but the best time to visit is from spring through fall for beach activities and hiking. Fall offers spectacular color hikes, and winter is ideal for sledding and cross-country skiing.

Operating Hours

The park is open daily from 8 AM to 10 PM throughout the year.

Entrance Fees:

- Michigan residents need a Recreation Passport for $12 annually.
- Non-residents can purchase a daily pass for $11 or an annual pass for $39

Your Digital Travel Companion
Scan to find recommended activities, digital guides, and beautiful images of this place.

🏔️ Natural Wonders & Parks | 📍 8800 M-116, Ludington, MI 49431

Ludington State Park

Ludington State Park, located between Hamlin Lake and Lake Michigan, offers a rich blend of natural beauty, including sand dunes, forests, and scenic beaches. The park spans 5,300 acres and is a favorite for outdoor activities like hiking, camping, and paddling. It is also home to the iconic Big Sable Point Lighthouse, one of Michigan's most photographed lighthouses.

Key Attractions:

- Big Sable Point Lighthouse: Accessible via a 1.8-mile trail, this historic lighthouse offers stunning views of Lake Michigan and the surrounding dunes.
- Hamlin Lake and Lake Michigan Beaches: The park features 7 miles of sandy shoreline along Lake Michigan and access to Hamlin Lake for fishing, boating, and swimming.
- Hiking Trails: With 21 miles of trails, including the popular Skyline Trail, visitors can explore the dunes, forests, and marshlands. Trails vary in

difficulty, providing options for both casual and experienced hikers

Best Time to Visit

Ludington State Park is open year-round, offering activities in every season. The best time for beachgoers and hikers is from May to October.

Operating Hours

The park is open from 8 AM to 10 PM daily, with campgrounds and other facilities observing quiet hours from 10 PM to 8 AM. The Big Sable Point Lighthouse is open for tours seasonally, typically from May through October.

Entrance Fees:

- Michigan Residents: A Recreation Passport is required for vehicle entry, costing $12 annually if purchased during vehicle registration, or $17 if purchased at the park.
- Non-Residents: A day pass costs $9, and an annual pass is $36.

Your Digital Travel Companion
Scan to find recommended activities, digital guides, and beautiful images of this place.

🏔 Natural Wonders & Parks | 📍 M-149, Manistique, MI 49854

Palms Book State Park (Kitch-iti-kipi)

Palms Book State Park, located in Michigan's Upper Peninsula, is home to one of the state's most stunning natural attractions, Kitch-iti-kipi, also known as "The Big Spring." This breathtaking freshwater spring spans 200 feet in diameter, is 40 feet deep, and pumps out more than 10,000 gallons of water per minute, maintaining a constant temperature of 45°F year-round. The crystal-clear water allows visitors to see fish and ancient tree trunks at the bottom, creating an otherworldly experience.

Key Attractions:

- Kitch-iti-kipi Observation Raft: Visitors can explore the spring aboard a self-operated raft that glides across the water. The raft is designed with a viewing hole, allowing visitors to observe the vibrant underwater world.
- Lush Forest Surroundings: The park is surrounded by beautiful forests and offers a serene atmosphere perfect for picnicking and relaxation.

Best Time to Visit

Palms Book State Park is open year-round, with Kitch-iti-kipi being particularly beautiful in all seasons. In winter, the snow-covered landscape adds to the park's charm. The spring's constant temperature keeps it ice-free, offering a unique winter experience.

Operating Hours

The park is open daily from 10 AM to 8 PM, making it easy to plan a visit at any time of the year.

Entrance Fees:

- Michigan Residents: A Recreation Passport is required for vehicle entry, costing $12 annually.
- Non-Residents: A day pass costs $9, or an annual pass is $36 for out-of-state visitors.

Your Digital Travel Companion
Scan to find recommended activities, digital guides, and beautiful images of this place.

Natural Wonders & Parks | Ocqueoc Falls Hwy, Presque Isle, MI 49759

Ocqueoc Falls

Ocqueoc Falls is Michigan's only publicly accessible waterfall in the Lower Peninsula, located in Presque Isle County. Known for its unique charm, the falls have a modest drop of about 5-10 feet over limestone bedrock, but their scenic beauty makes them a popular destination for families, nature lovers, and outdoor enthusiasts.

Key Attractions:

- The Waterfall: While not the largest in Michigan, Ocqueoc Falls is a great spot for swimming and wading during the summer months. It's especially known for its accessibility and is one of the few waterfalls that can be enjoyed up close by people of all abilities, thanks to the universally accessible paths.
- Bicentennial Pathway: A scenic hiking and biking trail system that winds through the surrounding forest and offers multiple loops ranging from 3 to 6 miles in length. It's perfect for hiking, mountain biking, and cross-country skiing in the winter.

Best Time to Visit

The best time to visit is during the warmer months (May through October) for swimming and hiking. Winter offers opportunities for snowshoeing and skiing along the pathway.

Operating Hours

The falls and park are open year-round, offering activities in every season.

Entrance Fees

A Michigan Recreation Passport is required for vehicle entry to the park. This costs $12 annually for Michigan residents or $9 daily for non-residents. An annual non-resident pass costs $36.

Your Digital Travel Companion
Scan to find recommended activities, digital guides, and beautiful images of this place.

🏔 Natural Wonders & Parks | 📍 Bond Falls Road, Paulding, MI 49912

Bond Falls

Bond Falls, located in Michigan's Upper Peninsula, is one of the state's most picturesque waterfalls. Created by the middle branch of the Ontonagon River, this waterfall cascades over volcanic rock in a series of breathtaking steps. With a total drop of about 50 feet and a width of 100 feet, Bond Falls is a must-visit destination for anyone exploring the western U.P.

Key Attractions:

- The Waterfall: Bond Falls features numerous small cascades that spread across a wide rocky area, offering multiple vantage points. It's particularly stunning during fall, when vibrant foliage surrounds the falls.
- Boardwalk and Viewing Areas: A 600-foot accessible boardwalk with six designated viewing platforms allows visitors to enjoy the falls from various angles, making it a great spot for photography.
- Picnic Areas: There are picnic spots near the trailhead, equipped with grills

and tables, making it a perfect place for a relaxed afternoon in nature.

Best Time to Visit

Bond Falls is open year-round, but it is particularly beautiful in the fall when the surrounding trees burst with color. Winter visitors can also enjoy the serene, frozen beauty of the falls.

Operating Hours

The site is open year-round. However, vehicle access is generally available from mid-May through mid-October, depending on weather conditions.

Entrance Fees:

A Michigan Recreation Passport is required for vehicle access to Bond Falls. For Michigan residents, an annual pass costs $12, while non-residents can purchase a day pass for $9 or an annual pass for $36.

Your Digital Travel Companion
Scan to find recommended activities, digital guides, and beautiful images of this place.

Natural Wonders & Parks | Porcupine Mountains Wilderness State Park, Carp Lake Township, MI 49953

Lake of the Clouds

Lake of the Clouds, located within the Porcupine Mountains Wilderness State Park in Michigan's Upper Peninsula, is one of the most iconic and scenic spots in the region. Set amidst ancient forests and rugged cliffs, this mountain lake offers visitors breathtaking views from an easily accessible overlook. It is especially popular for its stunning fall foliage and serene beauty throughout the year.

Key Attractions:

- Scenic Overlook: A short paved trail leads to the main overlook, which is fully accessible and offers sweeping views of the lake and surrounding wilderness. The view from here is one of the most photographed in Michigan, especially in fall when the forest bursts into vivid colors.
- Hiking Trails: Lake of the Clouds is surrounded by numerous trails, including the Big Carp River Trail and the Escarpment Trail, both of which provide more challenging hikes with unparalleled views of the lake and the surrounding Porcupine Mountains.
- Fishing: The lake is popular for bass fishing. It's catch-and-release only, and no boat rentals are available.

Best Time to Visit

The best times to visit are from late spring through fall, when the weather is most suitable for hiking and enjoying the scenery. Fall, in particular, offers stunning views as the surrounding forest turns vibrant shades of red, orange, and yellow.

Operating Hours

Porcupine Mountains Wilderness State Park, where Lake of the Clouds is located, is open year-round. The Porcupine Mountains Visitor Center operates from mid-May to mid-October.

Entrance Fees

A Michigan Recreation Passport is required for vehicle access. It costs $12 annually for Michigan residents and $9 daily for non-residents, with an annual pass option at $36 for non-residents.

Your Digital Travel Companion
Scan to find recommended activities, digital guides, and beautiful images of this place.

⛰ Natural Wonders & Parks | 📍 25970 Red Jacket Road, Calumet, MI 49913, USA

Keweenaw Peninsula

The Keweenaw Peninsula, located in Michigan's Upper Peninsula, is a stunning, remote region surrounded by the vast waters of Lake Superior. Known for its rich history and rugged landscapes, the Keweenaw offers a perfect blend of outdoor adventure, scenic drives, historical sites, and small-town charm. The area is famed for its copper mining heritage, lighthouses, waterfalls, and outdoor recreation.

Key Attractions:

- Copper Harbor: At the northern tip of the peninsula, Copper Harbor is the gateway to Isle Royale National Park and a hub for outdoor activities like hiking, mountain biking, and kayaking. The scenic Brockway Mountain Drive offers breathtaking views of Lake Superior, especially during the fall.
- Keweenaw National Historical Park: This park preserves the region's copper mining history. Visitors can tour sites such as the Quincy Mine and learn about the industry that shaped the Keweenaw.

- Lighthouses: The Keweenaw is home to several lighthouses, including Copper Harbor Lighthouse and Eagle Harbor Lighthouse, which provide insights into the area's maritime history.
- Waterfalls: The peninsula is dotted with beautiful waterfalls, such as Hungarian Falls and Eagle River Falls, offering scenic hiking opportunities.

Best Time to Visit

The best time to visit is summer (June through September), when temperatures are mild, and outdoor activities are in full swing. Fall is also a popular season due to the spectacular autumn foliage.

Entrance Fees:

For sites like Fort Wilkins State Park and other state-managed areas, a Michigan Recreation Passport is required, which costs $12 annually for residents or $9 per day for non-residents. Other activities such as lighthouse tours or historical site visits may have additional fees. The entrance to Keweenaw Peninsula is free.

Your Digital Travel Companion
Scan to find recommended activities, digital guides, and beautiful images of this place.

Natural Wonders & Parks | 📍 15310 N. Lighthouse Point Road, Northport, MI 49670

Leelanau State Park

Leelanau State Park, located at the tip of Michigan's Leelanau Peninsula, offers a serene escape into nature with over 1,550 acres of land featuring beautiful forested areas, rugged shorelines, and scenic views of Lake Michigan. The park is best known for its historic Grand Traverse Lighthouse, picturesque hiking trails, and rustic camping facilities.

Key Attractions:

- Grand Traverse Lighthouse: This iconic lighthouse, dating back to 1850, is one of the oldest on the Great Lakes. Visitors can tour the lighthouse for a small fee, climb to the top for panoramic views, and explore the museum, which showcases the history of Great Lakes shipping and lighthouse keeping.
- Cathead Bay Trails: The park has several miles of hiking trails, including the popular Cathead Bay Trail, which takes you through forested dunes and along the Lake Michigan shoreline,

offering great opportunities for birdwatching and photography.
- Camping: Leelanau State Park offers rustic camping with over 50 campsites, as well as mini cabins. The campground is quiet and peaceful, perfect for those looking to disconnect and enjoy nature. Note that the campground does not have modern amenities like showers or electricity, but vault toilets are available.

Best Time to Visit

Leelanau State Park is open year-round, but the best time to visit is from late spring to early fall when the weather is most pleasant for outdoor activities.

Operating Hours

The park is open daily from 8 AM to 10 PM.

Entrance Fees

A Michigan Recreation Passport is required for vehicle entry, costing $12 annually for residents and $9 daily for non-residents.

Your Digital Travel Companion
Scan to find recommended activities, digital guides, and beautiful images of this place.

Historical & Cultural Sites

Notes

Historical & Cultural Sites | 📍 20900 Oakwood Boulevard, Dearborn, MI 48124

The Henry Ford Museum of American Innovation

The Henry Ford Museum of American Innovation in Dearborn, Michigan, is a tribute to the greatest minds and inventions that have shaped the United States. It offers a deep dive into the country's industrial, cultural, and technological history, with immersive exhibits that engage visitors of all ages.

Key Attractions:

- The Rosa Parks Bus: Step inside the actual bus where Rosa Parks famously refused to give up her seat, sparking the civil rights movement.
- Automotive History: Explore the evolution of the automobile and its impact on American society in the "Driving America" exhibit.
- Aviation Innovations: Learn about the Wright brothers' achievements and advancements in aviation.
- Dymaxion House: Discover Buckminster Fuller's vision for

sustainable living in his futuristic Dymaxion House.

Operating Hours

The museum is open daily from 9:30 AM to 5:00 PM, except for Thanksgiving and Christmas

Entrance Fees:

- General Admission: $34 for adults, $30.50 for seniors (62+), and $25.50 for youth (5-11).
- Parking: There is a $9 parking fee per vehicle

Your Digital Travel Companion
Scan to find recommended activities, digital guides, and beautiful images of this place.

Historical & Cultural Sites | 📍 20900 Oakwood Boulevard, Dearborn, MI 48124

Greenfield Village

Greenfield Village is part of The Henry Ford complex in Dearborn, Michigan, and offers an immersive experience into 300 years of American history. Spread across 80 acres, this living history museum features authentic historic buildings, working farms, and skilled artisans. It transports visitors to different eras, showcasing the ingenuity and resourcefulness that shaped America.

Key Attractions:

- Historic Districts: The village is divided into seven districts, each representing different aspects of American life. Visitors can explore:

    a. Working Farms: Discover 19th-century farming techniques and meet farm animals.
    b. Liberty Craftworks: Watch artisans create glass, pottery, and more using period methods.
    c. Railroad Junction: Ride a steam-powered train and explore the 19th-century roundhouse.
    d. Edison at Work: Step into the lab where Thomas Edison invented the lightbulb.

Best Time to Visit

The village operates seasonally, typically from mid-April through the fall. The best time to visit is during warmer months to enjoy all the outdoor activities.

Operating Hours

Greenfield Village is open daily from 9:30 AM to 5:00 PM. Seasonal closures or special events may affect hours.

Entrance Fees:

- General Admission: $37 for adults, $33.25 for seniors (62+), and $27.75 for children (5-11). Children under 5 are free.
- Parking Fee: $9 per vehicle.

Your Digital Travel Companion

Scan to find recommended activities, digital guides, and beautiful images of this place.

Historical & Cultural Sites | 📍 Fort Mackinac, 7127 Huron Rd, Mackinac Island, MI 49757

Fort Mackinac

Fort Mackinac, located on Michigan's Mackinac Island, is a historic military outpost that offers visitors an immersive journey into the 18th and 19th centuries. Built by the British during the American Revolutionary War, the fort played a key role in military operations and later became a central hub of island life. Today, it's a beautifully preserved site that provides a glimpse into the past with costumed interpreters, interactive exhibits, and stunning views of the surrounding area.

Key Attractions:

- Cannon and Rifle Demonstrations: Daily demonstrations bring history to life with live cannon and rifle firings, marching soldiers, and hands-on drills that visitors can participate in.
- Historic Buildings: All 14 buildings within the fort are restored and open to the public. They include exhibits on military life, medical practices, and the history of the fort.
- Kids' Quarters: A hands-on exhibit where children can explore interactive games and activities related to the fort's history.
- Fire the Cannon: Visitors can make their trip extra special by participating in the iconic cannon firing.

Best Time to Visit

Fort Mackinac is open from May to late October, with the summer months being the best time for pleasant weather and full access to all activities and exhibits.

Operating Hours:

- May to early June: 9:00 AM to 5:00 PM
- June to early September: 9:30 AM to 7:00 PM
- September to mid-October: 9:30 AM to 5:00 PM.

Entrance Fees:

- Adults: $15.50
- Children (ages 5-12): $9.25
- Combination tickets that include other Mackinac Island attractions, such as Colonial Michilimackinac, are available for $28 for adults and $17 for children.

Your Digital Travel Companion
Scan to find recommended activities, digital guides, and beautiful images of this place.

Historical & Cultural Sites | 📍 461 Piquette Avenue, Detroit, MI 48202

The Ford Piquette Avenue Plant Museum

The Ford Piquette Avenue Plant in Detroit is a National Historic Landmark and the birthplace of the legendary Model T, the car that revolutionized transportation. Built in 1904, it was Ford's first purpose-built factory and is now a museum preserving this crucial piece of automotive history. Visitors can explore early automotive manufacturing and see rare cars from the early 20th century.

Key Attractions:

- Historic Exhibits: The museum houses over 65 vintage cars, including Ford's "Letter Cars" and early Model Ts. One of the highlights is the "Secret Experimental Room," where Henry Ford and his team designed the first Model T.
- Guided Tours: Knowledgeable guides provide 75-minute tours that cover the history of Ford's early innovations, the development of the Model T, and the factory's legacy.
- Self-Guided Tours: Visitors can also explore at their own pace, with

exhibits showcasing early manufacturing techniques and interactive displays.

Operating Hours:

- The museum is open Wednesday through Sunday, from 10:00 AM to 4:00 PM.
- The museum is closed on Mondays and Tuesdays and during major holidays such as Thanksgiving, Christmas, and July 4th.

Entrance Fees:

- Adults: $18
- Seniors (65+): $15
- Veterans 15$
- Students (with ID): $10
- Youth (5-17): $10
- Children (4 and under): Free
- Group tours are available for a discounted rate.

Your Digital Travel Companion
Scan to find recommended activities, digital guides, and beautiful images of this place.

Historical & Cultural Sites | 5200 Woodward Avenue, Detroit, MI 48202

The Detroit Institute of Arts (DIA)

The Detroit Institute of Arts (DIA), located in the heart of Detroit's cultural corridor, is one of the most significant art museums in the United States. With a collection of over 65,000 works, it covers a vast range of art from ancient to contemporary times, including masterpieces by artists like Van Gogh, Diego Rivera, and Rembrandt. The museum is also home to Rivera's "Detroit Industry" murals, considered one of the finest examples of 20th-century public art.

Key Attractions:

- Detroit Industry Murals: A series of 27 frescoes by Diego Rivera, which celebrate the automotive and labor industries of Detroit.
- Extensive Art Collection: The DIA showcases artwork from multiple periods and regions, including African, Asian, Native American, and European collections.
- Detroit Film Theatre: The museum features an on-site theater that hosts films, lectures, and special events.

Best Time to Visit

The museum is open year-round, with special exhibitions and events that change throughout the year. Visitors are encouraged to check the museum's calendar for details on upcoming exhibits and film screenings.

Operating Hours:

- Tuesday to Thursday: 9 AM to 4 PM
- Friday: 9 AM to 9 PM
- Saturday and Sunday: 10 AM to 5 PM
  The museum is closed on Mondays and major holidays, including New Year's Day, Independence Day, and Christmas Day.

Entrance Fees:

- General Admission: $20 for adults, $10 for seniors (65+) and students (with valid ID), and $8 for youth (ages 6-17). Children under 5 enter for free.
- Free Admission: Residents of Wayne, Oakland, and Macomb counties enjoy free general admission year-round with proof of residency.

Your Digital Travel Companion
Scan to find recommended activities, digital guides, and beautiful images of this place.

Historical & Cultural Sites | 📍 2648 W. Grand Blvd., Detroit, MI 48208

Motown Museum

The Motown Museum, located in Detroit, is famously known as Hitsville U.S.A., the birthplace of the Motown sound. It was here, in the home where Berry Gordy founded Motown Records in 1959, that legendary artists such as The Supremes, Stevie Wonder, and Marvin Gaye recorded their hits. Today, the museum offers an immersive experience, allowing visitors to step into the very studio where music history was made.

Key Attractions:

- Studio A: Experience the original recording studio where Motown's biggest hits were produced. Visitors can stand where iconic artists performed and recorded.
- Interactive Guided Tours: Each tour is led by knowledgeable guides who share captivating stories about the artists, producers, and staff who helped create the "Motown Sound." You'll also get to see Berry Gordy's apartment where he lived while establishing the label.

- Exhibits: Currently, the museum features the exhibit "Claudette Robinson: A Motown HER-story", celebrating the first lady of Motown, one of the original members of The Miracles.

Best Time to Visit

The museum is open Wednesday to Sunday, from 10 AM to 6 PM. On Saturdays, it stays open until 8 PM. It is closed on Mondays and Tuesdays, as well as major holidays such as Thanksgiving, Christmas Eve, and New Year's Day.

Entrance Fees:

- Adults: $20
- Seniors, Veterans, and Students: $17
- Children (5-17): $17
- Children under 4: Free

Your Digital Travel Companion
Scan to find recommended activities, digital guides, and beautiful images of this place.

Historical & Cultural Sites | 📍 303 Pearl St NW, Grand Rapids, MI 49504

Gerald R. Ford Presidential Museum

The Gerald R. Ford Presidential Museum in Grand Rapids, Michigan, offers visitors an in-depth look into the life and presidency of the 38th U.S. President, Gerald R. Ford. The museum presents permanent exhibits on his rise from a humble background to becoming president during one of the nation's most turbulent times. Visitors can explore displays of artifacts from his time in office, as well as First Lady Betty Ford's influential role. The museum also hosts temporary exhibits and educational programs that highlight Ford's legacy and key moments in American history.

Key Attractions:

- Permanent Exhibits: These feature a replica of the Oval Office during Ford's presidency, detailed displays of his political career, and reflections on major events like his controversial pardon of Richard Nixon.
- Temporary Exhibits: The museum regularly features rotating exhibits, such as "Ford at 50: Decisions that Defined a Presidency," which

commemorates the 50th anniversary of Ford's presidency.
- Betty Ford Garden and Gravesite: Visitors can pay respects at the burial site of President and Mrs. Ford, located on the museum grounds.

Best Time to Visit

The museum is open year-round, but visitors should check for specific events or exhibits. For example, the museum hosts special programs and celebrations on holidays like Independence Day.

Operating Hours:

- Monday to Saturday: 10 AM – 5 PM
- Sunday: 12 PM – 5 PM The museum is closed on major holidays such as Thanksgiving, Christmas, and New Year's Day.

Entrance Fees:

- Adults: $13
- Seniors (62+), Military Members: $11
- Youth (6-18): $7
- Children under 5: Free

Your Digital Travel Companion

Scan to find recommended activities, digital guides, and beautiful images of this place.

Historical & Cultural Sites | ⚲ 1000 E Beltline Ave NE, Grand Rapids, MI 49525

Frederik Meijer Gardens & Sculpture Park

Frederik Meijer Gardens & Sculpture Park, located in Grand Rapids, Michigan, is a unique blend of botanical gardens and art. Spanning 158 acres, it is home to one of the best outdoor sculpture collections in the world, featuring over 200 sculptures. The park offers a rich cultural experience through its blend of art, nature, and seasonal events, making it a must-visit destination in the Midwest.

Key Attractions:

- Sculpture Park: Recognized as one of the finest in the United States, it includes works from renowned artists like Auguste Rodin, Henry Moore, and Ai Weiwei.
- Indoor Gardens: The five-story, 15,000-square-foot Tropical Conservatory features exotic plants and butterflies in the spring. Other indoor attractions include arid, Victorian, and seasonal gardens.
- Japanese Garden: A peaceful, 8-acre traditional Japanese garden offering serene landscapes, waterfalls, and authentic Japanese design elements.
- Lena Meijer Children's Garden: A family favorite with interactive exhibits and fun for kids.

Best Time to Visit

Frederik Meijer Gardens is open year-round, with special seasonal events like the Butterflies Are Blooming exhibit in spring and the Holiday Traditions Around the World in winter.

Operating Hours:

- Sunday: 11 AM - 5 PM
- Monday, Wednesday, Thursday, Friday, Saturday: 9 AM - 5 PM
- Tuesday: 9 AM - 9 PM (Extended hours)

Entrance Fees:

- Adults (14-64): $20
- Seniors (65+), Students (with ID): $15
- Children (3-13): $10
- Children under 3: Free
- Museums for All program: $2 admission for qualifying visitors

Your Digital Travel Companion
Scan to find recommended activities, digital guides, and beautiful images of this place.

Historical & Cultural Sites | 5052 M-66, Charlevoix, MI 49720

Castle Farms

Castle Farms, located in Charlevoix, Michigan, was built in 1918 as a model dairy farm by the president of Sears, Roebuck & Co. It has since been beautifully restored and is now one of Michigan's premier historical attractions and a popular wedding venue. Visitors can enjoy exploring the castle's rich history, stunning gardens, and unique architectural features, offering a perfect day out for families and history enthusiasts alike.

Key Attractions:

- Model Railroad: Home to Michigan's largest outdoor model railroad, Castle Farms boasts over 70 trains running on more than 2,500 feet of track, a favorite for visitors of all ages.
- Gardens: The estate features 10 beautifully manicured Proven Winners gardens, each designed to showcase flowers that bloom throughout the year.
- WWI Museum: The 1918 Museum displays artifacts from the era, including items from the original Sears & Roebuck catalog and local memorabilia from World War I.
- Unique Exhibits: You'll find collections from castles around the world, a life-sized chess set, and even a friendly resident dragon named Norm.
- Guided and Self-Guided Tours: Visitors can choose between exploring the castle grounds on their own or joining a guided tour for in-depth stories about its fascinating history.

Best Time to Visit

The best time to visit is during the warmer months, from May to October, when the outdoor model railroad and gardens are fully operational. Castle Farms is open year-round, but hours may vary depending on the season.

Operating Hours:

- January - April: Tuesday to Saturday, 10 AM - 4 PM (closed Sundays and Mondays)
- May - October: Tuesday to Sunday, 10 AM - 4 PM (closed Mondays)
- November - December: Tuesday to Saturday, 10 AM - 4 PM (closed Sundays and Mondays)

Entrance Fees:

There are a variety of unique experiences available to book directly through their website. Simply scan the QR code below for instant access.

Your Digital Travel Companion
Scan to find recommended activities, digital guides, and beautiful images of this place.

🏰 Historical & Cultural Sites | 📍 500 Griswold St, Detroit, MI 48226

The Guardian Building

The Guardian Building, located in Detroit's Financial District, is one of the city's most iconic structures. Built in 1929, it is a premier example of Art Deco architecture, designed by Wirt C. Rowland. Nicknamed the "Cathedral of Finance," the building is famous for its vibrant tangerine-colored bricks, intricate tile work, and lavish interior decorations that blend Native American, Aztec, and Arts & Crafts influences. Today, it is both a National Historic Landmark and a functional office building.

Key Attractions:

- Lobby and Main Hall: The building's lobby features ornate murals, Pewabic Pottery tiles, and decorative metal screens that showcase the artistry of the time. The lobby is often considered one of the most visually stunning parts of the building.
- Architecture Tours: Visitors can take guided or self-guided tours to learn more about the building's design, history, and cultural significance. Tours offer insight into the detailed craftsmanship and the role of the Guardian Building in Detroit's development.
- Art Deco Design: The building's unique exterior, made of custom "Guardian Brick," and the intricate interior mosaic and marble work make it an architectural gem in downtown Detroit.

Operating Hours

The building is open for tours and visitors during regular office hours. Guided tours can be arranged through City Tour Detroit, with tours typically lasting around an hour.

Entrance Fees

General admission is around $6 for tours, which can be booked through the small gift shop located on the first floor.

Your Digital Travel Companion
Scan to find recommended activities, digital guides, and beautiful images of this place.

Historical & Cultural Sites | 830 Cottageview Drive, Suite 1011, Traverse City, MI 49684

The Village at Grand Traverse Commons

The Village at Grand Traverse Commons, located in Traverse City, Michigan, is a historic site that has been transformed into a vibrant community hub. Formerly the Traverse City State Hospital, this area is one of the largest historic preservation and adaptive reuse projects in the U.S. The village now features a mix of shops, restaurants, residential spaces, and trails, all set amidst beautiful historic architecture and expansive parkland.

Key Attractions:

- Historic Tours: Visitors can take guided tours of the former hospital buildings, including the iconic underground tunnels.
- Shopping & Dining: The Village is home to a variety of unique boutique shops and locally-owned restaurants. The historic Mercato shopping area is a highlight for those seeking artisanal goods and specialty foods.
- Botanic Garden: Visitors can explore the Botanic Garden at Historic Barns Park, which includes lush landscapes, trails, and gardens perfect for a leisurely stroll.
- Wine Tasting: Left Foot Charley, an on-site winery, offers wine tastings and a chance to relax while enjoying the beautiful surroundings.

Best Time to Visit

The Village is open year-round, but the best time to visit is during the warmer months when outdoor activities, gardens, and trails are at their best.

Operating Hours

Shops and restaurants in The Village typically operate from 10 AM to 6 PM, but individual businesses may vary in their hours..

Entrance Fees:

- There is no fee to explore the outdoor areas and shops at The Village.
- Guided tours of the historic buildings and tunnels are available.

Your Digital Travel Companion
Scan to find recommended activities, digital guides, and beautiful images of this place.

Historical & Cultural Sites | 📍 102 W Straits Ave, Mackinaw City, MI 49701

Colonial Michilimackinac

Colonial Michilimackinac, located in Mackinaw City, Michigan, is a historically reconstructed 18th-century fort and fur trading village. Originally built by the French in 1715 and later occupied by the British, the site offers visitors a glimpse into life in the Great Lakes region during the colonial era. The fort features historical reenactments, archaeological excavations, and interactive exhibits, making it a popular destination for families and history enthusiasts.

Key Attractions:

- Reenactments and Live Demonstrations: Daily programs include cannon and musket firings, cooking, blacksmithing, and other colonial-era crafts performed by costumed interpreters. These demonstrations vary throughout the day and immerse visitors in life during the 1700s.
- Historic Buildings and Exhibits: The fort consists of 16 reconstructed buildings with period-appropriate settings, such as the Commanding Officer's House, the Powder Magazine, and exhibits on fur trading and military life.
- Archaeological Dig: Witness one of the longest ongoing archaeological excavations in North America, where artifacts are still being uncovered each summer, providing insight into the fort's past.
- Kids' Rendezvous: A dedicated playground where children can learn about the fur trade and history in a fun, interactive way.

Best Time to Visit

The site is open seasonally from May to early October. Visitors will find the most activities during the peak summer months, from June to August, when live programs and archaeology digs are active.

Operating Hours:

- May to June: 9:00 AM – 5:00 PM
- June to September: 9:30 AM – 7:00 PM
- September to October: 9:30 AM – 5:00 PM Special events like the Fort Fright Halloween event extended hours during October.

Entrance Fees:

- Adults (13+): $15.25
- Children (5-12): $9.25
- Children under 5: Free Combination tickets that include nearby attractions, such as Old Mackinac Point Lighthouse or Fort Mackinac, are also available at discounted rates.

Your Digital Travel Companion
Scan to find recommended activities, digital guides, and beautiful images of this place.

Historical & Cultural Sites | 7029 Huron Road, Mackinac Island, MI 49757

Mackinac Island Historical Museum

The Mackinac Island Historical Museum offers a deep dive into the fascinating history of Mackinac Island, showcasing its development over the centuries from Native American settlements to a hub of fur trading and military significance. The museum, housed within Mackinac State Historic Parks, features several historic sites in the downtown area, making it an essential stop for visitors interested in the island's rich cultural heritage.

Key Attractions:

- Richard & Jane Manoogian Mackinac Art Museum: This museum is housed in the former Indian Dormitory and showcases an impressive collection of art inspired by Mackinac Island, along with historic artifacts.
- Biddle House & Native American Museum: Explore life on Mackinac Island in the 1820s and discover the stories of Native American women like Agatha Biddle.
- American Fur Co. Store & Dr. Beaumont Museum: This museum combines the history of the fur trade with Dr. Beaumont's medical research on digestion, which took place on Mackinac Island in the 1820s.

Best Time to Visit

The museum is open from May to October, with its peak season during the summer months. Special programs and events take place throughout the summer, including walking tours and historic reenactments.

Operating Hours

The museums generally operate from 10 AM to 5 PM during the open season, though some specific attractions may have varied hours.

Entrance Fees:

- Adults: $15.25
- Children (5-12): $9.25
- Children under 5: Free
- Combination tickets that include access to other attractions like Fort Mackinac are also available,

Your Digital Travel Companion
Scan to find recommended activities, digital guides, and beautiful images of this place.

Historical & Cultural Sites | ♥ 28123 Orchard Lake Road, Farmington Hills, MI 48334

Zekelman Holocaust Center

The Zekelman Holocaust Center, located in Farmington Hills, Michigan, is the state's premier Holocaust museum, dedicated to educating the public about the Holocaust and the dangers of hatred and prejudice. The 55,000-square-foot facility houses exhibits that include survivor testimonies, artifacts, and educational displays that provide a detailed account of this dark chapter in history, as well as a call to action for visitors to stand up against intolerance today.

Key Attractions:

- Permanent Exhibits: The museum's core exhibit highlights European Jewish life before, during, and after the Holocaust. Visitors will encounter artifacts, such as an original Holocaust-era boxcar used for deportations and a sapling from the tree that stood outside Anne Frank's hiding place.
- Special Exhibits: These focus on a variety of topics, including global genocides, Nazi persecution of marginalized groups, and heroic acts of resistance. A prominent exhibit, "Genocide in the East," covers the mass shootings that occurred in Eastern Europe during the Holocaust.
- Survivor Testimonies: The museum regularly features talks by Holocaust survivors from the local community, allowing visitors to hear first-hand accounts of resilience and survival.

Best Time to Visit

The museum is open Sunday through Friday, with shortened hours on Fridays due to observance of the Sabbath. Special

programming, including public tours led by docents, takes place every Sunday and Friday at 1:00 PM.

Operating Hours:

- Sunday to Thursday: 9:30 AM – 5:00 PM
- Friday: 9:30 AM – 3:00 PM
- Saturday: Closed The last admission is one hour before closing.

Entrance Fees:

- Adults: $8
- Seniors (62+) and College Students (with ID): $6
- Students (with ID): $5
- Free entry for uniformed service members, library visitors, and guests with EBT cards.

Your Digital Travel Companion
Scan to find recommended activities, digital guides, and beautiful images of this place.

Historical & Cultural Sites | 6865 W Hickory Road, Hickory Corners, MI 49060

The Gilmore Car Museum

The Gilmore Car Museum, located in Hickory Corners, Michigan, is one of the largest car museums in North America, boasting a collection of over 400 vintage and classic automobiles spread across a 90-acre campus. It features a blend of permanent and rotating exhibits, highlighting various eras and innovations in automotive history. The museum is a top destination for car enthusiasts and families alike, offering hands-on experiences like the Model T Driving Experience and vintage car rides.

Key Attractions:

- Exhibits: The museum has multiple themed exhibits, including "Celebrating 60 Years of the Ford Mustang" and displays covering different periods of automotive history.
- Vintage Rides: Visitors can experience rides in cars from the museum's collection, available seasonally from May through September.
- Model T Driving Experience: Learn to drive an authentic Ford Model T, guided by a museum expert, on the museum's grounds.
- Car Shows and Special Events: The museum hosts a variety of car shows, including muscle car meet-ups, vintage boat shows, and cruise-ins, especially during the summer season.

Best Time to Visit

The museum is open year-round, but the best time to visit is during the summer season (April to November), when all buildings and exhibits are open, and outdoor events are in full swing.

Operating Hours:

- Summer Season (April 1 - November 30):
    a. Monday to Friday: 9:00 AM – 5:00 PM
    b. Saturday & Sunday: 9:00 AM – 6:00 PM

- Winter Season (December 1 - March 31):
    c. Daily: 10:00 AM – 5:00 PM The museum is closed on major holidays like Easter, Thanksgiving, Christmas Eve, and Christmas.

Entrance Fees:

- Adults and Seniors: $20
- Youth (11-17): $12
- Children (10 and under): Free
- Veterans (with ID): $18
- Active Military (with ID): Free Two-day passes are available for $36 (adults).

Your Digital Travel Companion

Scan to find recommended activities, digital guides, and beautiful images of this place.

Iconic & Unique Attractions

Notes

🎷 Iconic & Unique Attractions | 📍 Mackinac Bridge Authority, N 415 I-75, St. Ignace, MI 49781

Mackinac Bridge

The Mackinac Bridge, connecting Michigan's Upper and Lower Peninsulas, is one of the world's longest suspension bridges, measuring 5 miles in total length. Completed in 1957, it spans the Straits of Mackinac, where Lake Michigan and Lake Huron meet. Known as the "Mighty Mac," it stands as an engineering marvel and one of Michigan's most iconic landmarks.

Key Attractions:

- Annual Mackinac Bridge Walk: Held on Labor Day each year, this event allows participants to walk the entire length of the bridge. It's a longstanding tradition since 1958, attracting tens of thousands of walkers annually.
- Bridge Tours and Events: Visitors can enjoy special events like vehicle parades for classic cars, tractors, and even snowmobiles that traverse the bridge.
- Scenic Drives: Driving across the bridge offers breathtaking views of the Great Lakes and surrounding landscapes, making it a favorite for tourists visiting the area.

Best Time to Visit

The Mackinac Bridge is open year-round, but the best time to visit is during the warmer months (May to October) when outdoor events like the Labor Day Bridge Walk are in full swing. Winter can be challenging due to potential closures caused by ice.

Entrance Fees:

- Passenger Vehicles: $4.00 per car
- Additional Fees: $2 per axle for trailers or RVs; larger vehicles like motorhomes or semi-trucks are charged $5 per axle.

Your Digital Travel Companion
Scan to find recommended activities, digital guides, and beautiful images of this place.

⚓ Iconic & Unique Attractions | 📍 2100 Woodward Avenue, Detroit, MI 48201

Comerica Park

Comerica Park is a renowned sports and entertainment venue located in downtown Detroit. Home to the Detroit Tigers, this ballpark combines the thrill of baseball with a family-friendly atmosphere, complete with a carousel, Ferris wheel, and stunning views of the Detroit skyline. Beyond baseball, Comerica Park hosts concerts and other events, making it a versatile venue for entertainment in the city.

Key Attractions:

- Baseball Games: As the home of the Detroit Tigers, Comerica Park regularly hosts Major League Baseball games during the season.
- Family-Friendly Features: Attractions include a carousel, Ferris wheel, and a large water feature in center field that is synchronized to music, offering fun for kids and families.
- Statues and Monuments: The park is adorned with statues of legendary Tigers players and a large tiger sculpture at the entrance, adding to the historic atmosphere.
- Concerts and Events: Comerica Park also serves as a concert venue for major performances, as well as hosting other sports and entertainment events.

Best Time to Visit

The park is busiest during the baseball season, from April to October, but it also hosts concerts and special events year-round.

Operating Hours

The stadium typically opens 1-2 hours before game time or event start time. Guided tours of the park are also available for $20 per person and provide behind-the-scenes access.

Entrance Fees:

- Game Tickets: Ticket prices vary depending on the event and seat location.
- Tours: $20 per person for a behind-the-scenes look at the park.

Your Digital Travel Companion
Scan to find recommended activities, digital guides, and beautiful images of this place.

🎷 Iconic & Unique Attractions | 📍 2000 Brush Street, Detroit, MI 48226, USA

Ford Field

Ford Field is a multi-purpose indoor stadium located in downtown Detroit, primarily serving as the home of the NFL's Detroit Lions. Opened in 2002, the stadium is known for its unique design, which incorporates a historic warehouse, and hosts a variety of sports events, concerts, and other large-scale activities. Located near Comerica Park and many downtown attractions, it is a hub for entertainment in the city.

Key Attractions:

- Detroit Lions Games: Ford Field is best known for hosting the Detroit Lions during the NFL season. The excitement of game day draws thousands of fans to experience the electric atmosphere.
- Concerts and Events: In addition to football, Ford Field is a major venue for concerts and special events, featuring performances from top international artists.
- Stadium Tours: Visitors can explore the stadium through guided tours that offer a behind-the-scenes look at the suites, locker rooms, and field access.

Best Time to Visit

Ford Field is a year-round venue. If you are visiting for a Detroit Lions game, the NFL season runs from September to January, with the playoffs extending into early February. Summer and fall also bring concerts and other events, making it a versatile destination for visitors.

Operating Hours

Hours vary depending on the event. For Detroit Lions games, gates typically open two hours before kickoff. Stadium tours are available year-round, but hours may vary by season, so it's best to check online in advance.

Entrance Fees

Ticket prices depend on the event. For Lions games, tickets are available through the NFL or secondary markets, with prices varying based on seat location and game demand. Stadium tour tickets can be purchased directly from the Ford Field website.

Your Digital Travel Companion
Scan to find recommended activities, digital guides, and beautiful images of this place.

⤵ Iconic & Unique Attractions | ⦿ Little Caesars Arena, 2645 Woodward Ave, Detroit, MI 48201

Little Caesars Arena

Little Caesars Arena, located in the heart of Detroit, is a modern multi-purpose venue that serves as the home for the NHL's Detroit Red Wings and the NBA's Detroit Pistons. Opened in 2017, it is a key part of "The District Detroit," a 50-block mixed-use development. The arena is renowned for its innovative design, with a massive glass-roofed concourse that mimics an outdoor street market, making it a year-round destination for sports and entertainment.

Key Attractions:

- Detroit Red Wings and Detroit Pistons Games: The arena is primarily home to these two major sports teams, making it a popular spot for hockey and basketball enthusiasts.
- Concerts and Shows: The venue also hosts world-class musical performances and events, having welcomed stars like Ariana Grande, Paul McCartney, and Post Malone.
- Dining Options: Inside, visitors can enjoy dining at venues such as Kid Rock's Made in Detroit or Mike's Pizza Bar.

Best Time to Visit

Little Caesars Arena is busy year-round, with the sports seasons running from October to April for hockey and basketball. Concerts and other events are held throughout the year.

Operating Hours

The XFINITY Box Office at the arena operates Monday to Friday from 11:00 AM to 5:30 PM, and on event days from 11:00 AM until 60 minutes after the event starts. For specific event times, it's best to check the arena's event schedule.

Entrance Fees

Ticket prices vary depending on the event. NHL and NBA games, as well as concerts, can be purchased directly through the arena or authorized resellers like Ticketmaster. Prices fluctuate based on seat location, event type, and demand.

Your Digital Travel Companion
Scan to find recommended activities, digital guides, and beautiful images of this place.

🎷 Iconic & Unique Attractions | 📍 8450 W. 10 Mile Road, Royal Oak, MI 48067

Detroit Zoo, Royal Oak

The Detroit Zoo, located in Royal Oak, just north of Detroit, spans 125 acres and houses over 2,400 animals representing 200 species. Opened in 1928, it was the first zoo in the United States to feature open, natural habitats, and it continues to be a leader in animal conservation and welfare. The zoo's diverse and immersive environments make it a perfect destination for families and wildlife enthusiasts alike.

Key Attractions:

- Polk Penguin Conservation Center: This award-winning exhibit houses four species of penguins in a state-of-the-art habitat that simulates Antarctic conditions, complete with a 25-foot-deep aquatic area where visitors can watch penguins swim.
- Arctic Ring of Life: One of the largest polar bear habitats in the world, this exhibit lets visitors observe polar bears and seals both above and below water.
- Giraffe Encounter: Visitors can get up close and personal with the zoo's giraffes, offering a unique opportunity to feed these gentle giants from an 18-foot-high platform.

Best Time to Visit

The zoo is open year-round, with longer hours from April through September (9:00 AM - 5:00 PM), and shorter hours from October through March (10:00 AM - 4:00 PM).

Operating Hours:

- April to September: 9:00 AM - 5:00 PM
- October to March: 10:00 AM - 4:00 PM
  The zoo is closed on Thanksgiving, Christmas, and New Year's Day.

Entrance Fees:

- Adults (19-64): $14 to $23
- Children (2-18) & Seniors (65+): $12 to $19
- Children under 2: Free Discounts are available for military personnel and groups. It is recommended to buy tickets online for the best price. .

Your Digital Travel Companion
Scan to find recommended activities, digital guides, and beautiful images of this place.

🎷 Iconic & Unique Attractions | 📍 4000 Baldwin Road, Auburn Hills, MI 48326

Great Lakes Crossing Outlets, Auburn Hills

Great Lakes Crossing Outlets is Michigan's largest indoor outlet mall, located in Auburn Hills, about 30 minutes north of Detroit. This 1.4 million-square-foot shopping and entertainment destination offers over 185 stores, restaurants, and attractions, making it an ideal stop for families, tourists, and bargain hunters alike.

Key Attractions:

- SEA LIFE Michigan Aquarium: Michigan's largest aquarium, offering a variety of marine life exhibits including interactive touch pools and a unique 180-degree underwater tunnel.
- LEGOLAND Discovery Center: Perfect for families, this attraction includes Lego-themed rides, a 4D cinema, and massive Lego creations, including a replica of downtown Detroit.
- Peppa Pig World of Play: A must-visit for younger children, this interactive indoor play area offers 14 themed attractions based on the beloved children's show.

Best Time to Visit

The mall is open year-round, making it a great destination in any season. To avoid crowds, consider visiting on weekday mornings. The busiest times are weekends and holidays, particularly around midday.

Operating Hours:

- Monday to Saturday: 10:00 AM – 9:00 PM
- Sunday: 11:00 AM – 6:00 PM.

Entrance Fees

There is no general entry fee to access the mall, but individual attractions like SEA LIFE Aquarium and LEGOLAND have their own admission fees. You can also purchase combo tickets to visit multiple attractions at a discounted rate.

Your Digital Travel Companion
Scan to find recommended activities, digital guides, and beautiful images of this place.

Iconic & Unique Attractions | 📍 925 S Main Street D-2, Frankenmuth, MI 48734

Frankenmuth River Place Shops

Frankenmuth River Place Shops is a charming Bavarian-themed outdoor shopping mall located in Michigan's "Little Bavaria," Frankenmuth. This unique destination offers more than 40 specialty shops, dining options, and family-friendly attractions, making it a perfect place for a day trip or a weekend getaway.

Key Attractions:

- Unique Shops and Boutiques: Explore a variety of stores offering everything from German-inspired gifts to handmade goods, fudge, and specialty foods.
- Bavarian Belle Riverboat: Take a scenic river cruise along the Cass River, offering beautiful views of Frankenmuth.
- Family-Friendly Activities: River Place Shops offers several seasonal events such as the Scarecrow Fest in the fall and 'Tis the Season Weekends during the holidays.
- Adventure Park: For those seeking excitement, the Adventure Park offers aerial obstacle courses that are suitable for all ages.

Best Time to Visit

The mall is open year-round, with special events throughout the year. Spring through fall is ideal for exploring the shops and attending outdoor festivals, while winter brings holiday-themed events. Heated sidewalks make the winter months more comfortable.

Operating Hours:

- January through May: Sunday to Thursday 11:00 AM – 6:00 PM, Friday and Saturday 11:00 AM – 8:00 PM.
- June: Sunday to Thursday 11:00 AM – 7:00 PM, Friday and Saturday 11:00 AM – 8:00 PM.
- July through September: Daily from 10:00 AM – 8:00 PM.
- September to December: Sunday to Thursday 11:00 AM – 6:00 PM, Friday and Saturday 11:00 AM – 8:00 PM.

Entrance Fees:

There is no general admission fee to access the shops. However, some attractions like the riverboat cruise or Adventure Park may have separate fees depending on the activity.

Your Digital Travel Companion

Scan to find recommended activities, digital guides, and beautiful images of this place.

Iconic & Unique Attractions | ♀ Somerset Collection, 2800 W Big Beaver Rd, Troy, MI 48084

Somerset Collection, Troy

Somerset Collection is Michigan's leading luxury shopping destination, located in Troy. The mall offers a blend of high-end and mid-tier stores, catering to a wide array of shoppers. It's renowned for its upscale shopping experience, with over 180 stores spread across two connected buildings, Somerset North and Somerset South.

Key Attractions:

- Luxury Retailers: Somerset Collection features top-tier brands such as Louis Vuitton, Gucci, Chanel, Hermès, Tiffany & Co., and more, offering a world-class shopping experience for luxury goods.
- Family-Friendly Stores: For families, stores like LEGO, Build-A-Bear Workshop, and the Apple Store are popular spots for both adults and kids.
- The Skywalk: A unique, glass-enclosed moving walkway connects Somerset North and South, adding a stylish architectural feature to the shopping experience.

Best Time to Visit:

Somerset Collection is open year-round. The mall tends to be quieter during weekdays, making it the ideal time for a relaxed shopping trip. Holiday seasons, especially Christmas, are festive and busier, with beautiful decorations and special events.

Operating Hours:

- Monday to Saturday: 10:00 AM – 8:00 PM

- Sunday: 12:00 PM – 6:00 PM

Entrance Fees:

There is no fee to enter Somerset Collection, and parking is also free. However, prices will vary depending on the stores and restaurants you visit.

Your Digital Travel Companion
Scan to find recommended activities, digital guides, and beautiful images of this place.

Iconic & Unique Attractions | 📍 25 Christmas Lane, Frankenmuth, MI 48734, USA ✈

Bronner's CHRISTmas Wonderland

Bronner's CHRISTmas Wonderland is the largest Christmas store in the world, located in Frankenmuth, Michigan. Open year-round, this iconic store spans 1.5 football fields and offers a staggering selection of over 50,000 holiday items, making it a must-visit for Christmas enthusiasts and families alike.

Key Attractions:

- Ornaments and Decorations: With an astonishing variety of ornaments, nativities, lights, and more, Bronner's caters to every holiday style, from traditional to modern. Personalized ornaments are a popular service, adding a special touch to any holiday keepsake.
- Silent Night Chapel: A replica of the famous Silent Night Chapel in Austria, this peaceful spot is open daily for visitors to enjoy reflection and meditation.
- Outdoor Christmas Lights: The half-mile-long Christmas Lane is illuminated with over 100,000 lights

every evening, creating a magical experience for visitors.

Best Time to Visit

Although Bronner's is open 361 days a year, the store is especially busy during the holiday season, particularly on weekends following Thanksgiving. For a quieter experience, consider visiting during weekdays or in the early fall when the festive ambiance begins but crowds are smaller.

Operating Hours:

- Monday to Saturday: 9:00 AM – 5:30 PM
- Sunday: 12:00 PM – 5:30 PM Bronner's is closed on New Year's Day, Easter, Thanksgiving, and Christmas Day.

Entrance Fees

There is no entry fee to visit Bronner's CHRISTmas Wonderland or the Silent Night Chapel. Some events and services, such as ornament personalization, may have additional costs.

Your Digital Travel Companion
Scan to find recommended activities, digital guides, and beautiful images of this place.

📍 Iconic & Unique Attractions | ● 6750 McGulpin Street, Mackinac Island, MI 49757, USA

The Original Mackinac Island Butterfly House & Insect World

Located on Mackinac Island, Michigan, The Original Mackinac Island Butterfly House is one of the oldest live butterfly exhibits in the U.S. and the first of its kind in Michigan. It features a tropical garden filled with hundreds of butterflies from four continents, offering a serene experience for visitors of all ages.

Key Attractions:

- Butterfly Garden: The main attraction is an 1800 sq. ft. tropical garden where over 1,000 butterflies freely fly, creating a magical atmosphere. The garden features an educational identification chart that helps visitors recognize different species of butterflies.
- Insect World: This section showcases some of the world's largest insects, including 14-inch walking sticks, giant beetles, and spiders. There's also a Nature Pond with fish, turtles, and

toads, making it a great educational experience for all ages.
- Butterfly Releases: Twice daily, newly emerged butterflies are released into the garden at 10:30 AM and 4:30 PM, which is a highlight for many visitors.

Best Time to Visit

The butterfly house is open seasonally, from mid-May through early October. Summer is an ideal time to visit Mackinac Island.

Operating Hours:

- Before Memorial Day & After Labor Day: 10:00 AM – 5:30 PM
- Memorial Day through Labor Day: 10:00 AM – 6:30 PM

Entrance Fees:

- Adults (12 & up): $14.00
- Children (5-11): $9.00
- Children (4 & under): Free

Your Digital Travel Companion
Scan to find recommended activities, digital guides, and beautiful images of this place.

🎷 Iconic & Unique Attractions | 📍 6151 Portage Road, Portage, MI 49002

Air Zoo Aerospace & Science Museum

The Air Zoo Aerospace & Science Museum in Kalamazoo is a Smithsonian-affiliated museum that offers a fascinating mix of aviation history, interactive science exhibits, and amusement park-style rides. It is a top destination for both aviation enthusiasts and families seeking a fun, educational day out. The museum showcases over 100 aircraft and spacecraft, hands-on STEM activities, and flight simulators, making it a unique experience that blends history with entertainment.

Key Attractions:

- Aircraft Exhibits: The museum houses a wide variety of aircraft, including those from early flight, World War II, the Jet Age, and the Space Age. Highlights include the iconic Lockheed SR-71 Blackbird, a P-38 Lightning, and a range of other warplanes and jets.
- Interactive Exhibits: Visitors can engage with STEM-focused exhibits like the "Women in Air & Space," which highlights female pioneers in aviation, and the "Alien Worlds & Androids" exhibit, exploring space technology and science fiction.
- Rides and Flight Simulators: The Air Zoo offers amusement rides, including the Flying Circus Biplane Ride and flight simulators that provide a thrilling, hands-on experience of what it's like to fly a plane.

Best Time to Visit

The Air Zoo is open year-round, making it a great destination at any time. However, weekdays tend to be less crowded, which may allow for a more relaxed experience.

Operating Hours:

- Monday to Saturday: 9:00 AM – 5:00 PM
- Sunday: 12:00 PM – 5:00 PM.

Entrance Fees:

- Adults (Ages 19-59): $18.00
- Seniors (60+): $15.00
- Children (Ages 5-17): $16.00
- Children (Ages 0-4): Free (no charge)

Your Digital Travel Companion
Scan to find recommended activities, digital guides, and beautiful images of this place.

 Iconic & Unique Attractions | 📍 1340 Atwater St, Detroit, MI 48207

Detroit International RiverWalk, Detroit

The Detroit International RiverWalk is a vibrant and scenic path that stretches over 3.5 miles along the Detroit River, offering breathtaking views of both the city's skyline and Windsor, Canada. This award-winning attraction has become a centerpiece for both locals and tourists, offering an array of recreational activities, parks, and historical landmarks.

Key Attractions:

- Cullen Plaza: A family-friendly spot featuring the Cullen Family Carousel with animals native to Michigan, as well as fountains and playgrounds. It's a great place for a relaxed stop along the walk.
- Milliken State Park and Lighthouse: This 31-acre park features a replica of the Tawas Point Lighthouse and is a perfect spot for a scenic break or photos.
- Robert C. Valade Park: A newer addition to the RiverWalk, this park offers a children's musical garden, playscapes, and the seasonal floating bar, Bob's Barge.
- Belle Isle Park: Located near the RiverWalk's eastern end, Belle Isle offers a conservatory, a nature center, and a beautiful park for a full day of exploration.

Best Time to Visit

The RiverWalk is open year-round and can be enjoyed in any season. However, the warmer months (late spring to early fall) are ideal for outdoor activities such as walking, cycling, and attending various events. Special events like the "Riverfront Run" in June and winter-themed weekends at

Valade Park provide added seasonal excitement.

Operating Hours

The RiverWalk is open daily from 6:00 AM to 10:00 PM, providing plenty of time to explore the scenic paths, parks, and attractions.

Entry Fees

Access to the Detroit International RiverWalk is free. Some activities, like bike rentals or visiting certain attractions, may have separate costs.

Your Digital Travel Companion

Scan to find recommended activities, digital guides, and beautiful images of this place.

Iconic & Unique Attractions | 3011 W. Grand Blvd., Detroit, MI 48202

The Fisher Building

The Fisher Building, located in Detroit's New Center area, is a renowned Art Deco skyscraper designed by the legendary architect Albert Kahn. Often referred to as "Detroit's Largest Art Object," the building opened in 1928 and stands 441 feet tall with a grand 28-story tower. It features an opulent interior filled with marble, mosaics, frescoes, and intricate details, making it a symbol of Detroit's architectural legacy.

Key Attractions:

- Art Deco Design: The Fisher Building is famous for its stunning Art Deco architecture, with a three-story barrel-vaulted arcade filled with hand-painted frescoes, brass fixtures, and marble sourced from across the globe.
- Fisher Theatre: This historic theater, located inside the building, has been a premier venue for Broadway shows and live performances since its renovation in 1961. The Fisher Theatre continues to host some of the top traveling Broadway productions.

- Shopping and Dining: The building houses a selection of boutique shops, a café, and other retailers, offering a unique shopping experience in a historic setting.

Best Time to Visit

The building is open year-round, but if you want to avoid crowds, weekdays are the best time for a more peaceful visit. There are also guided tours available, which offer a deeper look into its architecture and history.

Operating Hours

The Fisher Building is typically open from 8:00 AM to 6:00 PM on weekdays. The Fisher Theatre operates separately and may have extended hours depending on performance schedules.

Entry Fees

There is no fee to enter the Fisher Building. However, tickets are required for performances at the Fisher Theatre and for guided tours, which are offered for free by Pure Detroit.

Your Digital Travel Companion
Scan to find recommended activities, digital guides, and beautiful images of this place.

Detroit People Mover, Detroit

The Detroit People Mover is a fully automated light rail system that loops through downtown Detroit, covering a 2.9-mile elevated track. Launched in 1987, it is a convenient way for residents and tourists to explore the city's central attractions, including restaurants, hotels, and entertainment venues. It offers panoramic views of Detroit's skyline and waterfront as it connects 13 stations spread across the business district.

Key Attractions:

- Art in the Stations: Each of the People Mover's stations features unique artworks, including murals, sculptures, and mosaics created by renowned artists. For example, the Financial District Station features a mural by Joyce Kozloff inspired by Detroit's architectural icons, while Renaissance Center Station boasts a sculpture by Marshall Fredericks.
- Popular Stops: Key stops include Greektown (for its vibrant nightlife and restaurants), Renaissance Center

(headquarters of General Motors and access to the Detroit Riverwalk), and Huntington Place (Detroit's largest convention center).

Best Time to Visit

The People Mover operates year-round, but it is particularly useful during events such as sporting games at Little Caesars Arena or festivals at Hart Plaza. For a quieter experience and better sightseeing, weekdays and non-event times are recommended.

Operating Hours:

- Monday to Thursday: 7:00 AM – 10:30 PM
- Friday: 7:00 AM – Midnight
- Saturday: 10:00 AM – Midnight
- Sunday: 10:00 AM – 8:00 PM.

Entry Fees

For 2024, the Detroit People Mover is operating with free fare, allowing all passengers to ride at no cost as part of a pilot program.

Your Digital Travel Companion
Scan to find recommended activities, digital guides, and beautiful images of this place.

🎷 Iconic & Unique Attractions | 📍 Grand Hotel, 286 Grand Ave, Mackinac Island, MI 49757 ✈

The Grand Hotel, Mackinac Island

The Grand Hotel is an iconic landmark on Mackinac Island, known for its old-world charm, elegance, and historical significance. Opened in 1887, this magnificent hotel is home to the world's longest front porch, stretching 660 feet, and offers stunning views of the Straits of Mackinac. With its Victorian architecture and luxurious accommodations, the Grand Hotel transports visitors to a bygone era while providing modern amenities and exceptional service.

Key Attractions:

- The World's Longest Porch: The Grand Hotel's expansive front porch is a perfect place to relax, enjoy sweeping views of the island, and take in the charming ambiance.
- The Jewel Golf Course: A unique 18-hole course split between two locations, where players take a horse-drawn carriage between the front and back nine.
- Esther Williams Swimming Pool: A family-friendly pool named after the famous actress, perfect for a relaxing day.
- Secret Garden & Grounds: Explore beautifully manicured gardens, including a hidden Secret Garden that's a treat for those who discover it.

Best Time to Visit

The Grand Hotel is open from May through October, with summer being the most popular time due to the pleasant weather and many outdoor activities.

Operating Hours

The hotel operates seasonally from early May through late October. Non-hotel guests can visit daily from 9:00 AM to 6:00 PM for a self-guided tour, which costs $12 for adults and $6 for children.

Entry Fees

While staying at the Grand Hotel includes access to most facilities, non-guests can explore parts of the property, including the gardens and porch, for a fee of $12 per adult and $6 per child.

Your Digital Travel Companion
Scan to find recommended activities, digital guides, and beautiful images of this place.

🎷 Iconic & Unique Attractions | 📍 3 Inselruhe Avenue, Detroit, MI 48207

Belle Isle Aquarium

The Belle Isle Aquarium, located on Detroit's Belle Isle Park, is a historic attraction and one of the oldest public aquariums in the U.S., designed by famed architect Albert Kahn. Originally opened in 1904, the aquarium showcases a range of aquatic life with a focus on both freshwater and saltwater species. The building itself features beautiful green-tiled walls and arched ceilings, adding to its charm and historical significance.

Key Attractions:

- Unique Exhibits: The aquarium houses over 125 species, including fascinating creatures like garden eels, scorpion fish, and the critically endangered axolotl. There's also an invasive species exhibit, educating visitors on the environmental challenges facing the Great Lakes.
- Architectural Beauty: Beyond the fish and aquatic life, the aquarium itself is a stunning piece of architecture, with marble floors and unique Beaux Art design, reflecting the early 20th-century style.
- Conservation Education: The aquarium plays an important role in educating visitors about invasive species and conservation efforts to protect Michigan's waterways.

Best Time to Visit

Belle Isle Aquarium is open year-round, but it is only accessible Friday through Sunday from 10:00 AM to 4:00 PM. For a quieter experience, visiting in the morning is recommended.

Operating Hours:

- Friday to Sunday: 10:00 AM – 4:00 PM.

Entry Fees:

- Admission: Free, but donations are encouraged.
- Parking: Visitors will need a Michigan Recreation Passport, which costs $11 for cars. This passport provides access to all Michigan state parks.

Your Digital Travel Companion
Scan to find recommended activities, digital guides, and beautiful images of this place.

Scenic Drives & Trails

Notes

Scenic Drives & Trails | 📍 1100-3148, M-119, Harbor Springs, MI 49740

Tunnel of Trees (M-119)

The Tunnel of Trees is a renowned scenic drive along Michigan's M-119 highway, stretching about 20 miles from Harbor Springs to Cross Village. Hugging the Lake Michigan shoreline, this picturesque route is famous for its narrow, winding roads, breathtaking tree canopies, and charming small towns along the way. It's especially popular during the fall season when the trees turn vibrant shades of red, orange, and yellow, making it one of the most iconic drives in Michigan.

Key Attractions:

- Cross Village: At the northern end of the route, Cross Village is known for its historical significance and attractions like the Legs Inn, a rustic restaurant offering authentic Polish cuisine and stunning views of Lake Michigan. The village also features a Heritage Museum.
- Good Hart: This tiny town is home to the historic Good Hart General Store, which has been serving the community since the 1930s. Stop by for homemade baked goods, souvenirs, and famous pot pies. Don't miss the nearby art studios like Three Pines Studio and Gallery, and Good Hart Glassworks.
- Devil's Elbow: This infamous hairpin curve is steeped in local Native American legends. It's one of the more exciting points along the drive.

Best Time to Visit

The Tunnel of Trees is a year-round destination, but the best time to visit is during the fall (late September to mid-October) when the foliage is at its peak,

creating an unforgettable autumn display. Spring is another excellent time, with blooming wildflowers like trilliums covering the forest floor. Summer brings lush greenery and perfect weather for picnics and lake activities.

Operating Hours

The Tunnel of Trees is a public roadway and can be accessed anytime. However, it's best to drive during daylight hours to fully appreciate the views and safely navigate the winding roads.

Entry Fees

There is no entry fee for the Tunnel of Trees scenic drive itself. Some attractions along the way, such as Pond Hill Farm or Legs Inn, may have separate fees for food or activities.

Your Digital Travel Companion
Scan to find recommended activities, digital guides, and beautiful images of this place.

Scenic Drives & Trails | 📍 9922 Front Street, Empire, MI 49630

Pierce Stocking Scenic Drive

The Pierce Stocking Scenic Drive is a 7.4-mile loop through the breathtaking landscapes of Sleeping Bear Dunes National Lakeshore in Michigan. The drive takes visitors through a variety of environments, from lush forests to massive sand dunes, offering some of the most stunning views of Lake Michigan. It's one of the best ways to experience the natural beauty of the area, particularly for those short on time.

Key Attractions:

- Lake Michigan Overlook (Stop #9): This is one of the most popular spots on the drive, perched atop a 450-foot sand dune offering panoramic views of Lake Michigan. Visitors can also explore the nearby sand dunes but are advised not to descend the steep slopes due to the difficulty of climbing back up.
- Sleeping Bear Dune Overlook (Stop #10): Named after the legend of the Sleeping Bear, this overlook offers fantastic views of the dunes and the Manitou Islands in the distance.
- Glen Lake Overlook (Stop #2): This scenic spot provides beautiful views of Glen Lake, surrounded by vibrant forests and sand dunes.
- Beech-Maple Forest (Stop #7): A cool, shaded forest area where you can spot various wildlife including deer, chipmunks, and squirrels.

Best Time to Visit

The best time to experience the Pierce Stocking Scenic Drive is during late spring through fall. The fall months (late September to October) are particularly

stunning, as the forests transform into a colorful autumn display. However, the drive is equally beautiful in summer when you can enjoy warm weather and expansive views of the surrounding dunes and lakes.

Operating Hours

The drive is open daily from late May through mid-November, weather permitting. It operates from 9:00 AM until 30 minutes after sunset. In the off-season, the road is closed to vehicles but remains open to foot traffic.

Entry Fees

As part of Sleeping Bear Dunes National Lakeshore, a park pass is required. The fees are $25 per vehicle, valid for 7 days, or $45 for an annual pass. Passes can be purchased at the visitor center or the entrance.

Your Digital Travel Companion
Scan to find recommended activities, digital guides, and beautiful images of this place.

🥾 Scenic Drives & Trails | 📍 Trailhead located at Wilco Road, Empire, MI 49630

Empire Bluff Trail

Empire Bluff Trail is a 1.5-mile round-trip hike offering one of the most stunning views of Lake Michigan and Sleeping Bear Dunes. This moderately challenging hike takes you through beech-maple forests and sand dunes, ending at an elevated bluff about 400 feet above the lake. The trail is short but rewards visitors with panoramic views of Lake Michigan, South Bar Lake, and even the distant South Manitou Island.

Key Attractions:

- Scenic Overlook: The highlight of this hike is the overlook, where you can enjoy sweeping views of Lake Michigan and Sleeping Bear Dunes. It's a perfect spot for photography, picnics, or simply taking in the natural beauty of the area.
- Wildlife and Flora: The trail winds through a forest rich with wildlife and seasonal wildflowers like trillium, making spring and early summer particularly scenic.

- Geological Significance: The area is part of a perched dune system formed by glacial activity, offering a glimpse into Michigan's natural history.

Best Time to Visit

The trail is accessible year-round, but the best time to visit is between late spring and fall. Spring and summer provide pleasant hiking conditions with blooming wildflowers, while fall offers a spectacular display of colors as the leaves change.

Operating Hours

The trail is open 24 hours a day, but it's best to visit during daylight for safety and to fully appreciate the views. The trail remains open in winter, though icy conditions may make parts of the hike hazardous.

Entry Fees

As part of Sleeping Bear Dunes National Lakeshore, a $25 vehicle pass (valid for 7 days) is required to access the trail. This pass also covers other attractions in the area.

Your Digital Travel Companion
Scan to find recommended activities, digital guides, and beautiful images of this place.

🏃 Scenic Drives & Trails | 📍 Located near Copper Harbor, MI 49918

Brockway Mountain Drive

Brockway Mountain Drive is one of Michigan's most scenic routes, located in the Keweenaw Peninsula near Copper Harbor. Stretching for 9 miles along the ridge of Brockway Mountain, it offers breathtaking panoramic views of Lake Superior, inland lakes, and the surrounding forests. At 1,320 feet above sea level, it's the highest paved road between the Rockies and the Alleghenies, providing stunning vistas from various lookout points.

Key Attractions:

- Scenic Overlooks: The drive offers multiple scenic pull-offs with views of Lake Superior, Copper Harbor, and even Isle Royale on clear days. The West Bluff provides a 360-degree view that includes inland lakes such as Lake Medora and Lake Fanny Hooe.
- Birdwatching: Designated as a Michigan Wildlife Viewing Area, the drive is an excellent spot to watch the annual migration of birds of prey, particularly between mid-April and mid-June.
- Fall Colors: In autumn, Brockway Mountain becomes one of the best places in Michigan to witness vibrant fall foliage, with hues of red, orange, and yellow covering the landscape.

Best Time to Visit

The drive is open seasonally from April through November, with the fall months offering the most spectacular views of the changing leaves. Summer is another excellent time to visit for clear, sunny views of Lake Superior. The road is closed to vehicles in the winter, but snowmobiles can access the area.

Operating Hours

The drive is open daily from dawn to dusk during its operational season (April-November).

Entry Fees

There is no fee to drive along Brockway Mountain. The scenic drive and its overlooks are free and open to the public.

Your Digital Travel Companion

Scan to find recommended activities, digital guides, and beautiful images of this place.

🥾 Scenic Drives & Trails | 📍 51 Bailey Avenue, South Haven, MI 49090

Kal-Haven Trail

The Kal-Haven Trail is a 34-mile multi-use path connecting South Haven and Kalamazoo, Michigan. This former railroad corridor has been transformed into a scenic trail that passes through quaint towns, wooded areas, farmland, and wetlands. It's a favorite among hikers, cyclists, and outdoor enthusiasts who want to explore the natural beauty of southwest Michigan.

Key Attractions:

- Scenic Landscapes: The trail offers beautiful views of wildflower fields, forests, and streams. Along the way, you'll encounter historical bridges and small towns like Bloomingdale, where you can explore a small museum showcasing local history.
- Historical Markers: As part of its heritage designation, the Kal-Haven Trail includes 31 interpretive panels that highlight the history of the area, from former railroad towns to famous residents like boxing champion Joe Louis.

- South Haven: The trail ends at the shores of Lake Michigan in South Haven, providing access to South Beach and its historic lighthouse, perfect for cooling off on a hot day.

Best Time to Visit

The trail is accessible year-round, but the best time to visit is during late spring through fall. The summer months are perfect for biking and hiking, while fall offers a stunning display of autumn colors. Winter activities like cross-country skiing and snowmobiling are popular during the colder months.

Operating Hours

The trail is open year-round, and it's free to use. In the winter, snowmobilers will need a Michigan Snowmobile Permit.

Entry Fees

No entry fee is required to use the Kal-Haven Trail. However, if you plan to snowmobile during the winter, a Michigan Snowmobile Permit is needed.

Your Digital Travel Companion
Scan to find recommended activities, digital guides, and beautiful images of this place.

 Scenic Drives & Trails | 📍 7396 Market St, Mackinac Island, MI 49757

Mackinac Island Carriage Tours

Mackinac Island Carriage Tours is the world's largest and oldest horse-and-buggy livery, offering a charming way to explore Mackinac Island's historic and scenic spots. With motor vehicles banned on the island, horse-drawn carriages provide a nostalgic and relaxing way to tour this beautiful location. The tours are fully narrated, allowing visitors to learn about the island's rich history while enjoying its natural beauty.

Key Attractions:

- Surrey Hills Museum: The tour begins at this museum, which features historic carriages and artifacts. Here, visitors switch from a smaller two-horse carriage to a larger three-horse carriage for the main part of the tour.
- Arch Rock: One of the most iconic stops, Arch Rock is a natural limestone formation 146 feet above Lake Huron. The carriage stops here for visitors to take in the breathtaking views.
- Fort Mackinac: Another highlight, Fort Mackinac is a Revolutionary War-era fort where visitors can experience historical reenactments and explore 14 original buildings.
- Grand Hotel: The tour passes by the famous Grand Hotel, known for its grandeur and the world's longest porch. While the tour does not stop here, visitors can choose to end their tour at the hotel and explore its grounds.

Best Time to Visit

The tours operate from early May to late October, with the best time to visit being in the summer and fall months. Fall offers beautiful autumn colors, while summer brings lush greenery and warm weather.

Operating Hours:

- Early May to Mid-June: 9:00 AM – 5:00 PM
- Mid-June to Labor Day: 9:00 AM – 5:00 PM
- Labor Day to late September: 9:00 AM – 3:00 PM
- Early October to end of season: 9:00 AM – 2:00 PM.

Entry Fees:

- Traditional Carriage Tour: $39.50 for adults and $15.00 for children (5-12). Children under 4 are free if seated on a lap.
- Combination Ticket (Carriage Tour + Wings of Mackinac): $52.50 for adults, $23 for children.

Your Digital Travel Companion

Scan to find recommended activities, digital guides, and beautiful images of this place.

Scenic Drives & Trails | Old Mission Peninsula, Traverse City, MI 49686

Old Mission Peninsula Wine Trail

The Old Mission Peninsula Wine Trail stretches over 19 miles through the scenic Old Mission Peninsula in Traverse City, Michigan. Bounded by the crystal-clear waters of Grand Traverse Bay, the trail is home to ten wineries that produce exceptional wines, particularly Riesling, Pinot Grigio, and Chardonnay, thanks to the peninsula's cool climate. This trail is a paradise for wine lovers and those looking to enjoy a relaxing day surrounded by vineyards and breathtaking views.

Key Attractions:

- Chateau Chantal Winery and Inn: One of the standout stops, this winery offers stunning views of the bay and the vineyards, along with highly rated wines. It's a popular spot for both wine tasting and overnight stays.
- Brys Estate Vineyard & Winery: Known for its scenic Upper Deck overlooking the vineyard and the bay, as well as its picturesque lavender fields, Brys Estate offers a delightful experience for wine lovers.
- Bonobo Winery: This winery stands out with its rustic yet elegant atmosphere, live music, and popular wine-and-food pairings. Their smoked whitefish dip is a guest favorite.

Best Time to Visit

The best time to visit the Old Mission Peninsula Wine Trail is from late spring to fall, when the weather is warm, and the vineyards are lush. Fall is particularly beautiful as the leaves change colors, making the landscape even more picturesque. However, the wineries are open year-round, and winter visitors can enjoy more intimate experiences without the crowds.

Operating Hours

Most wineries are open daily, but hours can vary slightly depending on the season. Typically, tasting rooms are open from mid-morning to late afternoon or early evening. It's recommended to check individual wineries for exact times, especially in the off-season.

Entry Fees

Tasting fees vary by winery but generally range from $10 to $20 for a flight of wines. Some wineries, like 2 Lads Winery, offer more in-depth tasting experiences for around $40, which may include guided tours or wine-and-food pairings.

Your Digital Travel Companion
Scan to find recommended activities, digital guides, and beautiful images of this place.

🏃 Scenic Drives & Trails | 📍 Middleville, MI 49333,

North Country Trail (Michigan Section)

The Michigan section of the North Country Trail (NCT) covers over 1,100 miles, making Michigan the state with the most trail miles in the eight-state journey of the NCT. Stretching from the southern regions of the state up through both the Lower and Upper Peninsulas, it crosses through some of Michigan's most stunning landscapes, including national forests, lakeshores, and state parks.

Key Attractions:

- Pictured Rocks National Lakeshore: This section of the trail offers hikers the chance to explore Michigan's beautiful cliffs, waterfalls, and beaches along Lake Superior.
- Porcupine Mountains: Experience remote wilderness with breathtaking views and challenging terrains.
- Tahquamenon Falls State Park: Known for its majestic waterfalls, this park offers scenic hiking routes along the NCT.

Best Time to Visit

The trail is accessible year-round, with each season offering unique experiences. Summer and early fall are ideal for hiking, offering pleasant weather and, in autumn, incredible views of fall foliage. Winter attracts cross-country skiers and snowshoers looking for adventure in Michigan's snowy landscapes.

Operating Hours

The trail is open 24/7 year-round. However, certain sections that pass through state or national parks may have specific hours of operation, especially during winter or for overnight stays.

Entry Fees

There is no fee to hike the North Country Trail, but some sections of the trail, particularly those passing through Michigan State Parks or National Forests, may require parking or camping permits. For example, a Michigan Recreation Passport is required for entry into certain state parks and trailheads.

Your Digital Travel Companion
Scan to find recommended activities, digital guides, and beautiful images of this place.

🥾 Scenic Drives & Trails | 📍 41382 West M-123, Paradise, MI 49768

Tahquamenon Falls River Trail, Michigan

The Tahquamenon Falls River Trail is a scenic 4-mile trail that links the Upper and Lower Falls in Tahquamenon Falls State Park, one of Michigan's most famous natural attractions. The trail follows the Tahquamenon River, offering hikers views of beautiful waterfalls, lush forests, and abundant wildlife. It's considered one of the most rewarding, but also one of the more challenging trails in the park, due to its hilly terrain and exposed roots.

Key Attractions:

- Upper Falls: Known as one of the largest waterfalls east of the Mississippi River, the Upper Falls spans 200 feet and drops nearly 50 feet. Its unique amber color is caused by tannins from surrounding cedar and spruce swamps.
- Lower Falls: A series of five smaller cascading waterfalls surrounding an island. Rowboat rentals allow visitors to get up close to the falls and even hike the island.

- Old-Growth Forests: The trail winds through old-growth forests of maple, birch, and hemlock, providing a peaceful and immersive nature experience.

Best Time to Visit

The trail is open year-round, but the best time to visit is during the spring, summer, and fall months. Fall is particularly popular for the vibrant autumn colors. Winter hiking is also possible, although the trail is not maintained, and visitors may need snowshoes.

Operating Hours

The park is open from 8:00 AM to 10:00 PM, but hiking is best done during daylight hours to fully appreciate the scenery and safely navigate the trail. The shuttle service between the Upper and Lower Falls runs from Memorial Day through Labor Day.

Entry Fees

A Michigan Recreation Passport is required to enter the park, costing $12 for Michigan residents or $36 for non-residents. There are no additional fees to hike the trail itself.

Your Digital Travel Companion
Scan to find recommended activities, digital guides, and beautiful images of this place.

🥾 Scenic Drives & Trails | 📍 Belle Isle Park, Detroit, MI 48207

Iron Belle Trail

The Iron Belle Trail is Michigan's longest and most iconic trail system, extending over 2,000 miles from Detroit's Belle Isle to Ironwood in the Upper Peninsula. It is divided into two distinct routes: a hiking trail that stretches along the western side of the state, often using the North Country Trail, and a biking route that follows a different path on the eastern side, utilizing paved bike paths and country roads. The trail showcases Michigan's natural beauty and offers a diverse range of environments, from urban parks to remote forests and stunning waterfronts.

Key Attractions:

- Belle Isle Park: Starting point in Detroit, the park offers great views of the Detroit skyline and access to cultural attractions like the Belle Isle Aquarium.
- North Country National Scenic Trail: The hiking route includes portions of this scenic trail, offering wooded paths, streams, and rugged terrain.
- Pictured Rocks and Tahquamenon Falls: As you travel north into the Upper Peninsula, the trail passes near iconic Michigan destinations such as Pictured Rocks National Lakeshore and Tahquamenon Falls State Park.

Best Time to Visit

The trail is open year-round, but the best time to visit depends on the activities you plan to do. For hiking and biking, late spring through early fall offers the best weather, with autumn being particularly stunning due to the vibrant fall foliage. Winter opens up opportunities for snowshoeing and cross-country skiing in certain sections.

Operating Hours

The Iron Belle Trail is open 24 hours a day, year-round, though specific hours of access may vary depending on the section of the trail and local park regulations.

Entry Fees

Access to the trail is generally free, but some state parks or specific areas along the trail may require a Michigan Recreation Passport for parking or other amenities.

Your Digital Travel Companion
Scan to find recommended activities, digital guides, and beautiful images of this place.

 Scenic Drives & Trails |  Near Port Austin, MI 48467

Turnip Rock Kayak Trail

The Turnip Rock Kayak Trail is a popular 7-mile round-trip paddling route located in Lake Huron, starting from the small town of Port Austin. The highlight of this trail is Turnip Rock, a unique geological formation that has been sculpted by the lake's waves over thousands of years. The only way to access Turnip Rock is by water, making this kayak trail a favorite for adventure seekers and nature lovers alike.

Key Attractions:

- Turnip Rock: The star of the trail, this impressive rock formation stands isolated in the waters of Lake Huron, surrounded by crystal-clear waters.
- Sea Caves: Along the way, kayakers can explore smaller rock formations and sea caves that add to the adventure.
- Bird Creek Park: The starting point for many kayaking trips, this park offers a beach and picnic area, making it a great spot to begin and end your day

Best Time to Visit

The best time for kayaking to Turnip Rock is from late spring to early fall, with calm waters typically found in the summer months. It's advised to start early in the day to avoid wind and potential waves.

Entry Fees

There are no fees to access Turnip Rock, but kayak rentals are available in Port Austin starting at around $40 to $50 for the day. Parking fees may apply at launch sites like Bird Creek Park.

Your Digital Travel Companion
Scan to find recommended activities, digital guides, and beautiful images of this place.

Scenic Drives & Trails | 📍 PO Box 326, 350 Iron Street, Negaunee, MI 49866

Iron Ore Heritage Trail

Best Time to Visit

The trail is accessible year-round, but summer and fall provide the best weather for hiking and cycling. Winter activities, such as snowmobiling, are also popular along sections of the trail.

Entry Fees

There is no fee to use the trail itself, although some museums and attractions along the route may have separate entry fees.

The Iron Ore Heritage Trail is a 47-mile, multi-use trail that winds through Michigan's Upper Peninsula, celebrating the region's iron mining history. The trail stretches from Republic to Harvey, passing through key mining towns and offering educational exhibits along the way.

Key Attractions:

- Historical Markers: Throughout the trail, historical signs and displays highlight the region's rich mining heritage.
- Cliffs Shaft Mine Museum: Located in Ishpeming, this museum provides visitors with a deeper understanding of the iron mining process and its impact on the region.
- Scenic Vistas: The trail offers stunning views of forests, lakes, and former mining areas, giving hikers and cyclists a taste of the Upper Peninsula's rugged beauty.

Your Digital Travel Companion
Scan to find recommended activities, digital guides, and beautiful images of this place.

Scenic Drives & Trails | 📍 10781 E Cherry Bend Rd #1, Traverse City, MI 49684

Leelanau Peninsula Wine Trail

Nestled in the heart of northern Michigan, the Leelanau Peninsula Wine Trail is a celebrated route that weaves through the rolling hills and scenic landscapes of Leelanau Peninsula, offering wine enthusiasts a diverse array of local wineries to explore. Known for its picturesque vineyards, this trail is one of the most renowned wine regions in the Midwest, with a focus on cool-climate wines such as Rieslings, Chardonnays, and Pinot Noirs. Each winery offers its own unique atmosphere, with tasting rooms ranging from rustic and intimate to modern and expansive, all with breathtaking views of Lake Michigan.

Key Attractions:

- Wineries: The Leelanau Peninsula is home to over 25 wineries, each offering a unique selection of wines. Notable stops include Chateau de Leelanau, Leelanau Cellars, and Bel Lago Vineyards, where visitors can taste a variety of award-winning wines.
- Scenic Views: As you travel between wineries, enjoy stunning vistas of rolling vineyards, orchards, and the crystal-clear waters of Lake Michigan.
- Wine Events: The trail hosts seasonal events like "Harvest Stompede" in the fall and "Taste the Passion" during winter, offering a chance to experience the vineyards during Michigan's changing seasons.

Best Time to Visit:

The best time to visit is during the summer and fall, when the vineyards are in full bloom, and the weather is ideal for outdoor activities. Fall is particularly popular for its harvest season, with crisp air and vibrant autumn colors adding to the charm.

Operating Hours:

Each winery operates on its own schedule, with most opening around 11 AM to 6 PM. It's recommended to check individual winery hours, especially during off-season months, as hours may vary.

Entry Fees:

- Tastings: Wine tastings typically range from $5 to $15, depending on the winery and the selection of wines offered. Many wineries offer the fee toward the purchase of bottles.
- Tours: Guided wine tours, such as the Traverse City Leelanau Peninsula Wine Tour, include multiple tastings and transportation, with prices ranging from $100 to $150 per person.

Your Digital Travel Companion
Scan to find recommended activities, digital guides, and beautiful images of this place.

🥾 Scenic Drives & Trails | 📍 Starts from Empire, MI 49630

Sleeping Bear Heritage Trail

The Sleeping Bear Heritage Trail is a scenic, multi-use path that stretches through the heart of the Sleeping Bear Dunes National Lakeshore in northern Michigan. This 22-mile trail offers cyclists, hikers, and winter sports enthusiasts a unique way to experience the breathtaking landscapes of the lakeshore, which includes lush forests, sand dunes, and panoramic views of Lake Michigan. The trail is ideal for all ages and fitness levels, providing a leisurely yet immersive connection with nature. It also links several iconic points of interest within the national park, making it a great option for exploring the region's natural and cultural landmarks.

Key Attractions:

- Glen Haven Village: This historic village is a popular stop along the trail, offering a glimpse into Michigan's maritime past, with restored buildings and a museum showcasing the area's history.
- Dune Climb: A highlight for many visitors, the Dune Climb provides a challenging but rewarding trek up one of the towering sand dunes, with stunning views of Lake Michigan from the top.
- Pierce Stocking Scenic Drive: This 7.4-mile loop provides dramatic overlooks of the dunes, forests, and shoreline and is accessible via the trail. It's a must-see for anyone visiting the area.
- Crystal River: For those seeking a more leisurely activity, the Crystal River offers opportunities for kayaking and canoeing along a peaceful, meandering waterway near the trail.

Best Time to Visit:

The trail is accessible year-round, but the best times to visit are during the warmer months between May and October, when the trail is ideal for cycling, hiking, and walking. In the winter months, it transforms into a beautiful pathway for cross-country skiing and snowshoeing.

Operating Hours:

The Sleeping Bear Heritage Trail is open year-round, 24 hours a day. However, the best time for outdoor activities is during daylight hours, typically from 8 AM to dusk.

Entry Fees:

There is no fee to use the Sleeping Bear Heritage Trail itself, but visitors entering Sleeping Bear Dunes National Lakeshore must pay an entry fee:

- Private Vehicle: $25 (valid for 1-7 days)
- Motorcycle: $20
- Per Person (16+ years old): $15
- Annual Pass: $45 for unlimited access for a year

Your Digital Travel Companion
Scan to find recommended activities, digital guides, and beautiful images of this place.

Beach
Destinations

Notes

🏖 Beach Destinations | 📍 690 Perryman St, Saugatuck, MI 49453

Oval Beach

Oval Beach, located in Saugatuck, Michigan, is consistently ranked as one of the best beaches in the Midwest. Known for its pristine sandy shores, clear waters, and surrounding dunes, it offers visitors a serene and picturesque setting along the shores of Lake Michigan. Whether you're looking to relax on the soft sand, swim in the refreshing lake, or explore the nearby dunes, Oval Beach provides a quintessential Michigan beach experience that draws in locals and tourists alike

Key Attractions:

- The Beach: Oval Beach boasts a wide expanse of fine, soft sand perfect for sunbathing, playing volleyball, or building sandcastles. The water is typically calm, making it ideal for swimming.
- Mount Baldhead Park: A short distance from the beach, this park features a towering sand dune with 302 steps to the summit, offering panoramic views of Saugatuck, Lake Michigan, and the Kalamazoo River.

- Saugatuck Dunes State Park: Just a short drive away, this park offers hiking trails through the dunes and along the shoreline, perfect for those seeking more adventure.

Best Time to Visit:

The best time to visit Oval Beach is during the warm months of June through September.

Operating Hours:

Oval Beach is open year-round from 8 AM to 10 PM, but the prime season is during the summer months, when lifeguards are present and full facilities are operational.

Entry Fees:

- Daily Pass: $10 per vehicle (for Saugatuck Township residents, $6)
- Annual Pass: $50 per vehicle for unlimited access during the season
- Pedestrians and cyclists can enter for a $2 per person fee.

Your Digital Travel Companion
Scan to find recommended activities, digital guides, and beautiful images of this place.

Beach Destinations | 📍 60 Water St, South Haven, MI 49090, USA (South Beach and North Beach)

South Haven Beaches (South Haven Lighthouses)

Located on the shores of Lake Michigan, South Haven is home to some of the region's most beautiful and popular beaches. The South Haven Lighthouses, particularly the South Haven South Pierhead Light, is an iconic symbol of the area and a must-see for visitors. With soft sandy beaches, clear waters, and charming surroundings, South Haven is a prime destination for beachgoers, families, and anyone looking to enjoy Michigan's natural beauty. The town's picturesque lighthouses and rich maritime history add to the coastal charm, making it a top spot for relaxation, exploration, and stunning sunset views.

Key Attractions:

- South Beach: This beach offers a wide sandy area perfect for sunbathing, swimming, and playing beach volleyball. It's a family-friendly location with a playground, picnic areas, and easy access to nearby restaurants and shops.
- South Haven South Pierhead Light: This historic lighthouse, located on the south pier, is one of South Haven's most photographed landmarks. Visitors can walk along the pier, enjoy the stunning views of Lake Michigan, and take in the sunset.
- Maritime District: The area around the beach offers access to South Haven's Michigan Maritime Museum, which provides insights into the region's rich maritime heritage.

Best Time to Visit:

The best time to visit South Haven's beaches is during the summer months, from June to September, when the weather is warm, and the water is perfect for swimming. Early fall is also a great time to visit, with fewer crowds and pleasant temperatures.

Operating Hours:

South Haven's beaches are open year-round, though prime visiting hours are typically from 8 AM to dusk. During the summer, lifeguards are on duty at both North and South Beach to ensure safety.

Entry Fees:

- Beach Access: Free for pedestrians and cyclists.
- Parking Fees: $10 per vehicle during peak season (Memorial Day through Labor Day) at nearby parking lots.

Your Digital Travel Companion
Scan to find recommended activities, digital guides, and beautiful images of this place.

Beach Destinations | ♥ 1001 S Harbor Dr, Grand Haven, MI 49417

Grand Haven State Park

Grand Haven State Park, located on the eastern shore of Lake Michigan in Grand Haven, is a popular beach destination known for its stunning views, soft sandy shores, and the iconic Grand Haven Lighthouse and Pier. The park spans 48 acres and includes a beach, camping areas, and direct access to the pier, making it a favorite spot for both relaxation and outdoor recreation. The park's close proximity to downtown Grand Haven also offers easy access to shops, restaurants, and other attractions, making it a versatile destination for visitors.

Key Attractions:

- Grand Haven Beach: This wide, sandy beach is perfect for sunbathing, swimming, and picnicking. The soft sand and clean waters make it ideal for a day by the lake.
- Grand Haven South Pier and Lighthouse: The iconic red lighthouse and pier are major landmarks in the area. Visitors can walk along the pier, enjoy the views, and watch boats entering and leaving the Grand River.
- Grand Haven Musical Fountain: Just a short distance from the park, the Grand Haven Musical Fountain is a nightly light and water show set to music, providing entertainment for visitors of all ages.
- Sunset Views: Grand Haven State Park is renowned for its spectacular sunsets over Lake Michigan, attracting photographers and beachgoers who gather to witness the vibrant colors as the sun dips below the horizon.

Best Time to Visit:

The ideal time to visit Grand Haven State Park is during the summer months, from June to September, when the beach and lake are perfect for swimming, and the weather is warm and sunny.

Operating Hours:

The park is open year-round, 24 hours a day. However, facilities such as restrooms and concessions are generally available from 8 AM to 10 PM during the summer season.

Entry Fees:

- Daily Pass: Michigan residents can enter the park with a Recreation Passport for an annual fee of $18 per vehicle. For non-residents, the daily entry fee is $10 per vehicle.
- Camping: The park offers beachfront camping for both RVs and tents, with prices ranging from $33 to $45 per night, depending on the season.

Your Digital Travel Companion

Scan to find recommended activities, digital guides, and beautiful images of this place.

Beach Destinations | 📍 101 Broad St, St. Joseph, MI 49085

Silver Beach County Park

Silver Beach County Park, located in St. Joseph, Michigan, is a beloved beach destination along the eastern shore of Lake Michigan. Known for its soft, white sandy beach, crystal-clear waters, and family-friendly atmosphere, Silver Beach offers a perfect setting for a day of relaxation and fun. The park provides numerous amenities, including picnic areas, playgrounds, and access to the historic Silver Beach Carousel and the nearby St. Joseph North Pier Lighthouses, making it one of the most popular beach destinations in southwest Michigan.

Key Attractions:

- Silver Beach: The main attraction, Silver Beach offers a large, clean expanse of sandy shoreline, perfect for sunbathing, swimming, and playing beach volleyball. Lifeguards are on duty during the peak season, ensuring a safe environment for all visitors.
- St. Joseph North Pier and Lighthouses: A short walk from the beach, these historic lighthouses offer a scenic backdrop and a perfect place for photography, fishing, or simply enjoying the view.
- Silver Beach Carousel: Located adjacent to the park, this restored vintage carousel is a hit with families, offering a nostalgic ride for kids and adults alike.
- Shadowland Pavilion: This outdoor pavilion offers space for concerts and events, adding to the vibrant atmosphere of the park.

Best Time to Visit:

The best time to visit Silver Beach is during the summer months, from June to September, when the weather is warm, and the beach is perfect for swimming and sunbathing. Spring and early fall are also enjoyable times to visit, with fewer crowds and pleasant temperatures.

Operating Hours:

Silver Beach County Park is open year-round from 5 AM to dusk, with facilities and lifeguards typically available during the summer season from 10 AM to 6 PM.

Entry Fees:

- Vehicle Parking: $15 per vehicle during the peak season (May to September) for non-residents. St. Joseph residents can purchase discounted parking passes.
- Pedestrian and Cyclist Access: Free entry for those walking or biking into the park.

Your Digital Travel Companion
Scan to find recommended activities, digital guides, and beautiful images of this place.

Beach Destinations | 📍 1160 Broad Street, St. Joseph, MI 49085

St. Joseph Lighthouses

The St. Joseph Lighthouses are iconic landmarks located at the entrance of the St. Joseph River on the shores of Lake Michigan, in St. Joseph, Michigan. This duo of historic lighthouses, consisting of the St. Joseph North Pier Inner and Outer Lights, has guided sailors safely into the harbor since the early 20th century. Today, they stand as beloved symbols of the town and are popular attractions for visitors seeking beautiful views, historic charm, and picturesque sunsets over Lake Michigan.

Key Attractions:

- St. Joseph North Pier Outer Lighthouse: This tall, red-roofed lighthouse sits at the end of the North Pier, offering stunning views of Lake Michigan and the surrounding area. Visitors can walk along the pier to get up close to the lighthouse and enjoy a stroll over the water.
- St. Joseph North Pier Inner Lighthouse: Located closer to shore, this lighthouse is connected to the outer light via a long pier. The inner light is slightly shorter but equally charming, with a white structure and a matching red roof.
- Pier Walk: The concrete pier that connects the two lighthouses is a favorite spot for a leisurely walk, fishing, and sunset viewing. It offers panoramic views of Lake Michigan, the beach, and the town of St. Joseph.

Best Time to Visit:

The best time to visit the St. Joseph Lighthouses is during the warm months of May through October, when the weather is pleasant for outdoor activities, and Lake

Michigan's waters and skies create stunning backdrops for photos. Late summer and early fall are especially popular for sunset viewing.

Operating Hours:

The pier and lighthouse area are open to the public year-round, but access to the pier is safest and most enjoyable during daylight hours, from sunrise to sunset. Be cautious when visiting in the winter or during stormy weather, as the pier can become icy and dangerous.

Entry Fees:

- Access to the Pier and Lighthouses: Free for pedestrians. Visitors can walk along the pier to both the inner and outer lighthouses at no cost.
- Parking Fees: Parking near the beach and lighthouse area may require a small fee, especially during the peak summer season. Nearby Silver Beach County Park charges $15 per vehicle during the peak season.

Your Digital Travel Companion

Scan to find recommended activities, digital guides, and beautiful images of this place.

Beach Destinations | 📍 200 Marquette Dr, New Buffalo, MI 49117

New Buffalo Public Beach

New Buffalo Public Beach, located on the southern tip of Lake Michigan in New Buffalo, Michigan, is a favorite spot for visitors looking to enjoy a peaceful beach day. Known for its wide, sandy shoreline and calm waters, this beach offers a relaxing retreat for sunbathing, swimming, and enjoying the natural beauty of Lake Michigan. With nearby amenities, picnic areas, and a short walk to the charming town of New Buffalo, it's a convenient and scenic destination for families, couples, and beachgoers of all types.

Key Attractions:

- New Buffalo Beach: The beach itself features a large, clean stretch of soft sand perfect for lounging or playing beach games. The calm waters of Lake Michigan are ideal for swimming, and the beach is well-maintained, providing a peaceful environment.
- Dune Walk: A short dune trail near the beach offers visitors a scenic walk with panoramic views of the beach and lake, perfect for photography or a quiet moment of reflection.
- Boating and Water Sports: The adjacent harbor makes this a popular destination for boaters, and visitors can rent kayaks, paddleboards, or jet skis nearby for some fun on the water.
- Proximity to Downtown: The beach is just a short walk from downtown New Buffalo, where visitors can explore local restaurants, shops, and the harbor area, making it easy to spend a full day in the area.

Best Time to Visit:

The best time to visit New Buffalo Public Beach is during the warm summer months from June to September, when the weather is perfect for swimming, sunbathing, and water activities. Early autumn is also a lovely time to visit, with fewer crowds and pleasant weather for beach walks.

Operating Hours:

New Buffalo Public Beach is open from 6 AM to 11 PM daily. It's a great place to spend the day, with lifeguards typically on duty during peak season hours, from 10 AM to 6 PM.

Entry Fees:

- Parking Fees: There is a fee for parking near the beach, typically $15 per vehicle during the peak summer months. It's recommended to arrive early during weekends and holidays, as parking can fill up quickly.

Your Digital Travel Companion

Scan to find recommended activities, digital guides, and beautiful images of this place.

Beach Destinations | 8660 Lake St, Gary, IN 46403,

Lake Michigan Beach Park

Lake Michigan Beach Park is a hidden gem located in the small town of Empire, Michigan, along the eastern shores of Lake Michigan. This beautiful park offers stunning views of Lake Michigan's blue waters and sandy beaches, making it an excellent spot for beachgoers, nature lovers, and families looking for a quieter alternative to busier beaches. With its natural beauty, calm atmosphere, and access to the famous Sleeping Bear Dunes National Lakeshore, this park is an ideal destination for those wanting to explore Michigan's breathtaking shoreline while enjoying a peaceful day at the beach.

Key Attractions:

- Lake Michigan Beach: The park's wide, sandy beach is perfect for relaxing, sunbathing, or taking a peaceful stroll along the shoreline. The clear waters are great for swimming, and the beach is less crowded compared to other Lake Michigan destinations.
- Scenic Views of Sleeping Bear Dunes: From the beach, you can enjoy views of the towering Sleeping Bear Dunes in the distance, a unique and picturesque backdrop for your day at the lake.
- Access to Sleeping Bear Dunes: The park is close to some of the best hiking and dune climbing spots in the Sleeping Bear Dunes National Lakeshore, offering visitors the opportunity to explore both the beach and the surrounding natural beauty.

Best Time to Visit:

The best time to visit Lake Michigan Beach Park is during the summer months, from June to September, when the weather is ideal for swimming and beach activities. Early fall is also a great time to visit, as the weather remains pleasant, and the park is less crowded, offering a peaceful and scenic experience.

Operating Hours:

Lake Michigan Beach Park is open year-round, but the prime visiting hours for beach activities and picnicking are typically from 8 AM to dusk during the summer months.

Entry Fees:

- Entrance to the Beach: Free for pedestrians and cyclists.
- Parking Fees: There may be a small parking fee of around $10 per vehicle during peak season, depending on local regulations and enforcement.

Your Digital Travel Companion

Scan to find recommended activities, digital guides, and beautiful images of this place.

Beach Destinations | 📍 3510 Channel Dr, Muskegon, MI 49441

Pere Marquette Park (Muskegon)

Pere Marquette Park, located in Muskegon, Michigan, is a popular beach park situated along the eastern shores of Lake Michigan. Known for its expansive sandy beach, iconic Muskegon South Pierhead Light, and excellent amenities, it's a favorite destination for both locals and visitors. With ample space for swimming, picnicking, beach volleyball, and water sports, Pere Marquette Park provides a perfect setting for a day of fun and relaxation by the lake. The park's close proximity to Muskegon's downtown and other attractions makes it a versatile and convenient getaway.

Key Attractions:

- Pere Marquette Beach: This large, pristine beach offers soft sand and crystal-clear waters, ideal for swimming, sunbathing, and playing beach games. The beach is also great for walking and relaxing by the water.
- Muskegon South Pierhead Light: Located at the southern end of the beach, this historic red lighthouse is one of Muskegon's most iconic landmarks. Visitors can walk along the pier, take photos, or enjoy fishing from the pier.
- Lighthouses Tour: The Muskegon South Breakwater Light offers tours during the summer months, allowing visitors to climb to the top for stunning views of Lake Michigan and the surrounding coastline.

Best Time to Visit:

The best time to visit Pere Marquette Park is during the warm summer months, from June to September, when the weather is perfect for swimming, sunbathing, and enjoying the beach activities. Late spring and early fall are also pleasant times to visit, with fewer crowds but still beautiful conditions for beach walks and outdoor recreation.

Operating Hours:

Pere Marquette Park is open year-round, with the beach accessible from 5 AM to 10 PM daily. During the summer months, lifeguards are on duty during prime swimming hours, typically from 11 AM to 7 PM.

Entry Fees:

- Beach Access: Free entry for pedestrians and vehicles, making it an accessible and budget-friendly destination.
- Parking Fees: Parking is free at Pere Marquette Park, with plenty of space available near the beach and picnic areas.

Your Digital Travel Companion
Scan to find recommended activities, digital guides, and beautiful images of this place.

🏖 Beach Destinations | 📍 Empire, MI 49630,

Empire Beach

Empire Beach, located in the quaint village of Empire, Michigan, is a picturesque destination along the shores of Lake Michigan. This peaceful beach offers stunning views of both Lake Michigan and the Sleeping Bear Dunes National Lakeshore, making it a favorite spot for nature lovers and beachgoers alike. With its wide sandy shoreline, playgrounds, picnic areas, and nearby dunes, Empire Beach is a perfect destination for families, couples, and anyone looking to enjoy the natural beauty of the Great Lakes.

Key Attractions:

- Empire Beach: The wide, sandy beach is ideal for swimming, sunbathing, and relaxing. The clean, clear waters of Lake Michigan make it a refreshing spot for a dip during the summer months.
- Empire Bluff Trail: Just a short drive from the beach, this popular hiking trail offers breathtaking panoramic views of Lake Michigan and the surrounding landscape from atop the dunes.
- Playground and Picnic Areas: Empire Beach is equipped with a playground, making it a family-friendly destination, and there are several picnic areas where visitors can enjoy a meal while taking in the lake views.
- Sunsets: Empire Beach is renowned for its stunning sunsets over Lake Michigan. Many visitors come in the evening to witness the sky transform into vibrant shades of orange, pink, and purple.

Best Time to Visit:

The best time to visit Empire Beach is during the summer months, from June to September, when the weather is perfect for swimming, hiking, and beach activities. Early fall is also a great time to visit for cooler temperatures and beautiful autumn foliage in the surrounding area.

Operating Hours:

Empire Beach is open year-round, with the best time for beach activities between 8 AM and dusk. The beach is accessible all day, but lifeguards are typically on duty only during peak summer months.

Entry Fees:

- Beach Access: Free for pedestrians and cyclists.
- Parking Fees: There is a nominal fee for parking, usually around $1 per hour or $5 per day, making it an affordable option for a day at the beach.

Your Digital Travel Companion

Scan to find recommended activities, digital guides, and beautiful images of this place.

Beach Destinations | 6400 Main St, Caseville, MI 48725

Caseville Beach

Caseville Beach, located in the charming town of Caseville, Michigan, is a popular destination on the eastern shore of Saginaw Bay, which is part of Lake Huron. Known for its wide, sandy shoreline, shallow waters, and family-friendly atmosphere, Caseville Beach offers a relaxing environment for both locals and visitors. The beach is one of the central attractions in Caseville, which is also famous for its annual Cheeseburger in Caseville Festival, celebrating the town's love for burgers, fun, and the laid-back, "beach town" lifestyle.

Key Attractions:

- Caseville Beach: The main attraction, this beach provides a soft sandy shore and calm, shallow waters, making it perfect for families with young children and those looking to enjoy a swim or paddle.
- Cheeseburger in Caseville Festival: Held every August, this Jimmy Buffett-inspired festival is one of Michigan's most famous summer events. During the festival, Caseville Beach becomes a hub for visitors enjoying beachside activities, live music, and, of course, burgers.
- Saginaw Bay Views: The beach offers stunning views of Saginaw Bay and the waters of Lake Huron, perfect for a relaxing day by the lake or a peaceful walk along the shore.
- Caseville Harbor: Adjacent to the beach is the Caseville Harbor, where visitors can watch boats coming in and out or enjoy water sports, such as kayaking and boating.

Best Time to Visit:

The best time to visit Caseville Beach is during the summer months, from June to September, when the weather is warm and the water is perfect for swimming. The beach is particularly lively during the Cheeseburger in Caseville Festival in August, making it an exciting time to visit.

Operating Hours:

Caseville Beach is open daily from 8 AM to 10 PM, allowing visitors to enjoy the beach throughout the day, from early morning walks to evening sunsets.

Entry Fees:

- Beach Access: Free for pedestrians.
- Parking Fees: Parking near the beach is typically free, though during events like the Cheeseburger Festival, there may be limited space, so it's advisable to arrive early.

Your Digital Travel Companion
Scan to find recommended activities, digital guides, and beautiful images of this place.

⚓ Beach Destinations | 📍 4490 Beach Rd, Cheboygan, MI 49721

Cheboygan State Park Beach

Cheboygan State Park Beach, located within Cheboygan State Park in Michigan's northern Lower Peninsula, offers a serene and scenic retreat on the shores of Lake Huron. Known for its peaceful atmosphere, clear waters, and breathtaking views of the Straits of Mackinac, the beach is perfect for those looking to enjoy a quiet day by the lake. The park also features several trails, opportunities for wildlife viewing, and access to the Fourteen Foot Shoal Lighthouse, making it a great destination for nature lovers and outdoor enthusiasts.

Key Attractions:

- Cheboygan State Park Beach: This quiet, sandy beach offers a tranquil spot for swimming, sunbathing, and picnicking along the shores of Lake Huron. The waters are typically calm, making it ideal for families and those looking for a peaceful experience.
- Fourteen Foot Shoal Lighthouse Views: From the beach, you can see the Fourteen Foot Shoal Lighthouse, located off the coast in Lake Huron. The lighthouse adds to the scenic beauty of the area, making it a popular spot for photography.
- Hiking and Nature Trails: The park is home to several hiking trails that wind through forests, wetlands, and along the lakeshore. These trails offer opportunities to explore the natural landscape and spot local wildlife, including birds, deer, and more.
- Camping: Cheboygan State Park offers both rustic and modern campsites, allowing visitors to extend their stay and enjoy more time in the great outdoors.

Best Time to Visit:

The best time to visit Cheboygan State Park Beach is during the summer months, from June to September, when the weather is warm enough for swimming and other outdoor activities. Early fall is also a pleasant time to visit, with cooler temperatures and fewer crowds, making it perfect for hiking and enjoying the autumn colors.

Operating Hours:

The park and beach are open year-round, with the best hours for beach activities typically from 8 AM to dusk during the summer months.

Entry Fees:

- Daily Park Pass: Michigan residents can enter the park with a Recreation Passport for an annual fee of $18 per vehicle. Non-residents must pay a $10 daily entry fee or can purchase an annual pass for $36.

Your Digital Travel Companion
Scan to find recommended activities, digital guides, and beautiful images of this place.

Beach Destinations | 📍 99 Pleasure Dr, Detroit, MI 48207,

Belle Isle Beach (Detroit)

Belle Isle Beach, located on Belle Isle Park in the heart of Detroit, Michigan, offers a scenic and relaxing getaway along the Detroit River. This island park, situated between the U.S. and Canada, is a favorite spot for both locals and visitors looking to enjoy outdoor activities, with the beach being a major attraction. The beach provides a refreshing escape from the urban environment, offering swimming, sunbathing, and spectacular views of the Detroit skyline and the Canadian shore. Belle Isle Park is also home to several other notable attractions, making it a diverse and vibrant destination.

Key Attractions:

- Belle Isle Beach: The sandy beach is ideal for a day of swimming and sunbathing, with shallow waters perfect for wading and cooling off during the summer months. The beach area is well-maintained and family-friendly.
- Views of the Detroit Skyline: From the beach, visitors can enjoy stunning views of the Detroit skyline across the river, offering a unique city-meets-nature experience.
- Belle Isle Fountain: The James Scott Memorial Fountain is a stunning marble fountain that serves as a central feature of the island and is a popular spot for photos.

Best Time to Visit:

The best time to visit Belle Isle Beach is during the summer months, from June to September, when the weather is warm and perfect for beach activities. Summer also brings numerous events and festivals to

Belle Isle Park, adding to the lively atmosphere.

Operating Hours:

Belle Isle Beach is open from 5 AM to 9 PM, with peak visiting hours during the daytime. Lifeguards are typically on duty during the summer months, from 10 AM to 8 PM, ensuring a safe environment for swimmers.

Entry Fees:

- Park Access: Michigan residents can enter Belle Isle Park with the Recreation Passport, which costs $18 annually per vehicle. Non-residents must pay a $9 daily entry fee.
- Parking: Free parking is available throughout Belle Isle Park, including near the beach area.

Your Digital Travel Companion
Scan to find recommended activities, digital guides, and beautiful images of this place.

Beach Destinations |  201 E River Road, Oscoda, MI 48750

Oscoda Beach Park

Oscoda Beach Park, located along the shores of Lake Huron in Oscoda, Michigan, is a charming and family-friendly destination known for its expansive sandy beach, picturesque lake views, and vibrant atmosphere. The park serves as a beloved gathering spot for both locals and visitors, offering a perfect mix of relaxation and recreation on the Great Lakes.

Key Attractions:

- Sandy Beach: The wide, clean beach stretches along Lake Huron, providing ample space for sunbathing, picnicking, or just lounging with a book. The shallow waters make it safe for swimming, and the lake's calm waves are perfect for families with children.
- Pier and Boardwalk: A wooden boardwalk runs along the park, offering a scenic walking route with beautiful lake views. The pier is ideal for a leisurely stroll or fishing, with benches available for those wanting to take in the peaceful surroundings.
- Playground and Pavilion: The park features a modern playground that will delight children of all ages. There's also a spacious pavilion equipped with picnic tables and barbecue grills, making it perfect for family gatherings or casual cookouts.
- Water Sports: Kayaking and paddleboarding are popular activities here, with calm waters that are perfect for beginners and casual paddlers alike.
- Historic Lighthouse Replica: Oscoda Beach Park is home to a replica of the area's historic lighthouse, which

makes for a great photo spot and adds a touch of local history to the experience.

Best Time to Visit:

The best time to visit Oscoda Beach Park is between late spring and early fall (May to September). Summer months bring warm temperatures ideal for swimming, while the fall offers cooler, more peaceful settings with the bonus of fall colors along the shoreline.

Operating Hours:

Oscoda Beach Park is open year-round, but peak visiting times are during the warmer months. While the park itself is accessible 24 hours a day, the pavilion and playground may have specific operating hours during off-peak seasons.

Entry Fees:

There are no entry fees to access Oscoda Beach Park, making it an affordable and accessible destination for visitors.

Your Digital Travel Companion
Scan to find recommended activities, digital guides, and beautiful images of this place.

Beach Destinations | 📍 5th Ave Beach, Manistee, MI 49660

Manistee North Pierhead Lighthouse

The Manistee North Pierhead Lighthouse, located on the shores of Lake Michigan in Manistee, Michigan, is a quintessential example of Great Lakes maritime history. This iconic lighthouse, standing proudly at the end of a picturesque pier, has been guiding ships into the harbor since the late 1800s. Visitors are drawn to its rich history, scenic views, and its beautifully preserved structure, making it a must-see destination for anyone exploring Michigan's west coast.

Key Attractions:

- The Lighthouse: The lighthouse itself is a striking steel tower, painted white, with a distinctive black lantern room on top. Although the lighthouse is no longer operational, it remains an important symbol of the area's maritime heritage and is a favorite subject for photographers, especially at sunrise or sunset.
- The Pier: Stretching out into Lake Michigan, the pier offers stunning panoramic views of the lake, the Manistee River, and the surrounding shoreline. It's perfect for a leisurely walk, with the sound of the waves and the breeze adding to the peaceful atmosphere.
- Historic Catwalk: The Manistee North Pier is also known for its unique catwalk, a structure that extends from the lighthouse back to the shore.
- Lake Michigan Views: The surrounding area offers beautiful views of Lake Michigan's endless blue waters, making it a peaceful spot to relax, watch boats, or take in a spectacular sunset.

Best Time to Visit:

The best time to visit the Manistee North Pierhead Lighthouse is from May to October. During these months, the weather is warm, and the views are particularly stunning, especially during summer sunsets. Fall visits also offer beautiful autumn colors along the lake's shoreline.

Operating Hours:

The lighthouse and pier are accessible year-round, though visitors should be mindful of weather conditions, especially during the winter months when the pier can be icy and dangerous. Summer months provide the best access to the pier and surrounding areas.

Entry Fees:

There is no fee to access the Manistee North Pierhead Lighthouse and pier. Visitors can freely explore the area and take in its historic charm.

Your Digital Travel Companion
Scan to find recommended activities, digital guides, and beautiful images of this place.

⚓ Beach Destinations | 📍 3582 State Park Dr, Bay City, MI 48706

Bay City State Park Beach

Bay City State Park Beach, located along the Saginaw Bay shoreline in Bay City, Michigan, offers visitors a peaceful retreat with its expansive sandy beach, natural beauty, and diverse recreational activities. This serene spot is part of Bay City State Park, a 2,000-acre nature preserve that is home to wetlands, woodlands, and Saginaw Bay's refreshing waters. It is a haven for nature lovers, families, and outdoor enthusiasts looking for a scenic getaway in central Michigan.

Key Attractions:

- Sandy Beach: The long stretch of beach offers soft sand and calm waters, making it perfect for a relaxing day in the sun.
- Saginaw Bay: The bay provides stunning views and is ideal for water-based activities. Its calm waters make it perfect for kayaking, paddleboarding, and fishing, while the surrounding scenery offers a picturesque backdrop for a day at the beach.
- Tobico Marsh: Adjacent to the beach is Tobico Marsh, a wetland area rich in wildlife and perfect for birdwatching. The marsh features hiking trails and observation towers, providing a great opportunity to explore the area's natural habitats.
- Wildlife and Nature Programs: Bay City State Park offers various educational programs and activities, such as guided nature walks and talks, especially during the summer months. It's an excellent way to learn more about the local ecosystem.

Best Time to Visit:

The best time to visit Bay City State Park Beach is between May and September. Summer offers warm weather perfect for swimming, sunbathing, and other beach activities. Spring and fall are also great for hiking and birdwatching, with the cooler temperatures making for comfortable outdoor adventures.

Operating Hours:

Bay City State Park Beach is open year-round from 8 AM to 10 PM. While the beach is accessible year-round, lifeguards are only on duty during the summer season, typically from Memorial Day through Labor Day.

Entry Fees:

A Michigan Recreation Passport is required for vehicle entry into Bay City State Park:

- Michigan Residents: $13 annually (added to vehicle registration) or $18 for a day pass.
- Non-residents: $39 annually or $10 for a day pass.

Your Digital Travel Companion

Scan to find recommended activities, digital guides, and beautiful images of this place.

Beach Destinations | Sleeping Bear Dunes National Lakeshore, Empire, MI 49630

Sleeping Bear Bay Beach

Sleeping Bear Bay Beach, located within the Sleeping Bear Dunes National Lakeshore along the scenic shores of Lake Michigan, is one of Michigan's most breathtaking and serene beach destinations. Nestled in the heart of the park, this beach offers visitors stunning views of the iconic Sleeping Bear Dunes, crystal-clear waters, and a tranquil atmosphere. It's a perfect place for both relaxation and outdoor adventure in one of Michigan's most picturesque settings.

Key Attractions:

- Sleeping Bear Dunes: The beach is framed by the towering Sleeping Bear Dunes, which rise dramatically above the shoreline. These massive dunes, formed by centuries of wind and water erosion, provide a stunning backdrop and a unique experience for visitors.
- Manitou Islands View: On clear days, you can see the distant Manitou Islands from the beach, adding to the sense of wonder and natural beauty. These islands are part of local Anishinaabe legends and play an important role in the area's cultural heritage.
- Hiking Trails: Nearby hiking trails provide access to the dunes and surrounding natural areas, including the famous Dune Climb and various scenic overlooks, offering panoramic views of Sleeping Bear Bay and Lake Michigan.
- Historic Sites: The area around Sleeping Bear Bay Beach also includes historical landmarks, such as the Glen Haven Historic Village, a

restored 19th-century village that offers a glimpse into Michigan's maritime past.

Best Time to Visit:

The best time to visit Sleeping Bear Bay Beach is between May and October. During the summer months, the weather is perfect for swimming, sunbathing, and exploring the dunes.

Operating Hours:

The beach and the surrounding park areas are open year-round, but the peak season for beach activities is during the warmer months.

Entry Fees:

Entry to Sleeping Bear Dunes National Lakeshore requires a pass:

- Private Vehicle: $25 (valid for 1-7 days)
- Motorcycle: $20
- Per Person (16+ years): $15
- Annual Pass: $45 for unlimited visits within one year

Your Digital Travel Companion

Scan to find recommended activities, digital guides, and beautiful images of this place.

Wineries & Breweries

Notes

Wineries & Breweries | 📍 15900 Rue de Vin, Traverse City, MI 49686,

Chateau Chantal Winery & Tasting Room

Chateau Chantal Winery & Tasting Room, located on the beautiful Old Mission Peninsula in Traverse City, Michigan, offers a one-of-a-kind wine tasting experience with panoramic views of rolling vineyards, the blue waters of Grand Traverse Bay, and a charming French chateau atmosphere. This family-owned winery is known for its award-winning wines, scenic setting, and warm hospitality, making it a must-visit destination for wine enthusiasts and those looking for a relaxing getaway.

Key Attractions:

- Winery and Vineyard Tours: Chateau Chantal offers guided tours of their vineyards and winemaking facilities, giving visitors an insider's look at the winemaking process. Learn about the region's unique terroir, grape varietals, and the careful craftsmanship that goes into each bottle of wine.
- Tasting Room: The tasting room at Chateau Chantal provides a wide selection of wines to sample, from crisp whites like Chardonnay and Riesling to robust reds like Merlot and Pinot Noir, as well as sweet and dessert wines.
- Wine Dinners: Chateau Chantal hosts regular wine dinners, offering gourmet, multi-course meals paired with their estate wines. These events are perfect for a special night out or celebrating a special occasion.

Best Time to Visit:

- The best time to visit Chateau Chantal is from May to October when the weather is warm, and the vineyards are lush and green. Summer and fall are particularly popular times to visit due to the winery's stunning views and outdoor seating areas.

Operating Hours:

Chateau Chantal Winery & Tasting Room is open year-round, but hours may vary by season:

- Summer (May–October): Open daily from 11 AM to 6 PM.
- Winter (November–April): Open daily from 11 AM to 5 PM. Reservations are recommended, especially during the busy summer months and on weekends.

Entry Fees:

There is no fee to enter the winery, but tastings and tours come with costs:

- Wine Tastings: Prices vary depending on the number of samples, typically ranging from $10 to $15 per person.
- Tours: Guided tours are often offered for an additional fee and may include wine tastings.

Your Digital Travel Companion

Scan to find recommended activities, digital guides, and beautiful images of this place.

 Wineries & Breweries | 📍 3309 Blue Water Road, Traverse City, MI 49686

Brys Estate Vineyard & Winery

Brys Estate Vineyard & Winery, located on the scenic Old Mission Peninsula in Traverse City, Michigan, is a family-owned winery known for its handcrafted wines, picturesque vineyard views, and warm hospitality. Set on 111 acres of rolling vineyards, the estate offers a tranquil and elegant atmosphere where guests can enjoy wine tastings, vineyard tours, and exclusive experiences, all while soaking in the stunning scenery of Grand Traverse Bay.

Key Attractions:

- Wine Tasting Room: The tasting room at Brys Estate is a cozy and inviting space where visitors can sample a selection of the winery's award-winning wines. Varietals include Riesling, Chardonnay, Cabernet Franc, Merlot, and their signature Pinot Noir, among others. The outdoor deck offers a perfect spot for sipping wine while enjoying panoramic views of the vineyards and Lake Michigan.
- Secret Garden: One of the unique features of Brys Estate is the Secret Garden, a charming space filled with vibrant flowers, lavender fields, and fresh herbs. Visitors can stroll through the garden, take in the delightful fragrances, and even purchase locally made lavender products like oils, lotions, and bath salts from the garden's shop.
- Vineyard Tours: The winery offers guided vineyard tours where guests can learn about the grape-growing process, the unique terroir of the Old Mission Peninsula, and the estate's winemaking practices.

Best Time to Visit:

The best time to visit Brys Estate is between May and October.

Operating Hours:

Brys Estate is open year-round, with hours varying by season:

- Spring & Summer (May–October): Open daily from 11 AM to 6 PM.
- Fall & Winter (November–April): Open daily from 11 AM to 5 PM.

Reservations are recommended, particularly during peak tourist season in the summer.

Entry Fees:

There is no fee to enter Brys Estate Vineyard & Winery, but wine tastings and other experiences have associated costs:

- Wine Tastings: Typically $10–$15 per person, which includes a selection of wine samples..

Your Digital Travel Companion
Scan to find recommended activities, digital guides, and beautiful images of this place.

🍾 Wineries & Breweries | 📍 8175 Center Rd, Traverse City, MI 49686

Mari Vineyards

Mari Vineyards, located on the scenic Old Mission Peninsula in Traverse City, Michigan, is a standout destination for wine lovers seeking a refined yet welcoming experience. This family-owned winery is renowned for its commitment to producing high-quality, Italian-inspired wines, grown in its estate vineyards overlooking Grand Traverse Bay. With its modern architecture, spectacular views, and diverse wine offerings, Mari Vineyards provides a unique and memorable visit for guests exploring Michigan's wine country.

Key Attractions:

- Tasting Room: The impressive stone-clad tasting room at Mari Vineyards is both modern and rustic, providing a beautiful setting for sampling their carefully crafted wines. The indoor tasting space has large windows offering stunning views of the vineyards and Grand Traverse Bay, while outdoor seating is available for those who want to soak in the fresh air.
- Wines: Known for producing Italian-style wines, Mari Vineyards offers a diverse selection of varietals that are uncommon in the region, such as Nebbiolo, Sangiovese, and Refosco. Their flagship wine, "Ultima Thule," is a red blend that showcases the estate's dedication to Old World winemaking techniques.
- Underground Barrel Cellar: One of the most unique features of Mari Vineyards is its 3,000-square-foot underground barrel cellar. Dug into the hillside, this space is used for aging wine and is a must-see for

visitors interested in the winemaking process.

Best Time to Visit:

The best time to visit Mari Vineyards is from May to October.

Operating Hours:

Mari Vineyards is open year-round, but the hours vary by season:

- Spring & Summer (May–October): Open daily from 11 AM to 6 PM.
- Fall & Winter (November–April): Open daily from 11 AM to 5 PM. Entry Fees:

There is no fee to enter the winery, but tastings and tours have associated costs:

- Wine Tastings: Typically $10–$15 per person, depending on the number of wines tasted.
- Tours: Guided tours, including a visit to the underground barrel cellar, range from $20–$25 per person and usually include a wine tasting.

Your Digital Travel Companion

Scan to find recommended activities, digital guides, and beautiful images of this place.

Wineries & Breweries |  185 Mt. Tabor Road, Buchanan, MI 49107,

Tabor Hill Winery

Tabor Hill Winery, located in the picturesque rolling hills of Buchanan, Michigan, is one of the region's oldest and most beloved wineries. Known for its award-winning wines, culinary experiences, and scenic setting, Tabor Hill Winery has been a staple in Michigan's wine country for over 50 years. The combination of wine tasting, dining, and breathtaking vineyard views makes it a must-visit destination for both wine connoisseurs and those looking for a relaxing day in a beautiful environment.

Key Attractions:

- Tasting Room: The elegant tasting room at Tabor Hill offers visitors the chance to sample a wide variety of their wines, from classic dry whites and reds to sweet dessert wines and sparkling selections.
- Restaurant: Tabor Hill is known for its on-site restaurant, which features farm-to-table cuisine crafted to pair perfectly with their wines. Guests can enjoy a gourmet meal while overlooking the vineyards. The seasonal menu includes locally sourced ingredients, offering a true taste of Michigan wine country.
- Wines: Tabor Hill produces a range of wines, including popular varietals such as Chardonnay, Pinot Grigio, Cabernet Franc, and Merlot. Their award-winning demi-sec wines are particularly well-known, offering a sweeter, more approachable option for those new to wine tasting.

Best Time to Visit:

The best time to visit Tabor Hill Winery is from late spring to early fall.

Operating Hours:

Tabor Hill Winery is open year-round, but hours vary by season:

- Spring & Summer (May–October): Open daily from 11 AM to 6 PM.
- Fall & Winter (November–April): Open daily from 12 PM to 5 PM. Reservations are recommended, especially for the restaurant and guided tours, during busy seasons and weekends.

Entry Fees:

There is no fee to enter the winery, but wine tastings and tours come with costs:

- Wine Tastings: Tastings generally range from $10 to $15 per person, depending on the selection of wines.
- Vineyard Tours: Private vineyard tours, which include a detailed explanation of the winemaking process and tastings, are typically available for $20–$25 per person.

Your Digital Travel Companion

Scan to find recommended activities, digital guides, and beautiful images of this place.

Wineries & Breweries | 10983 Hills Road, Baroda, MI 49101

Round Barn Winery

Round Barn Winery, located in Baroda, Michigan, is a unique and vibrant destination that offers much more than just wine tasting. Known for its iconic Amish-built round barn, this family-owned estate has become a favorite spot for visitors seeking a fun and relaxing experience in Southwest Michigan's wine country. Round Barn Winery is part of the Moersch Hospitality Group and offers a diverse range of beverages, including wine, craft beer, and spirits, making it an all-in-one stop for drink enthusiasts and families alike.

Key Attractions:

- Iconic Round Barn: The winery's namesake and centerpiece is its historic round barn, which dates back to 1881. The barn's architecture is not only visually striking but also serves as a unique venue for tastings, events, and gatherings. It's a one-of-a-kind setting that offers a memorable experience for visitors.
- Wine, Beer, & Spirits Tasting: Round Barn offers tastings of its award-winning wines, craft beers, and spirits. From their signature red and white wines to their popular fruit wines and distilled spirits like vodka and whiskey, there's something for everyone to enjoy. Guests can opt for a flight or individual tastings depending on their preferences.
- Brewing Company & Public House: In addition to the winery, Round Barn also features its own brewery. Beer lovers can enjoy craft brews made on-site, including seasonal and small-batch varieties. The Public House, located nearby, serves wood-fired

pizzas and other delicious dishes, making it a perfect place to relax with food and drinks.

Best Time to Visit:

The best time to visit Round Barn Winery is from late spring to early fall.

Operating Hours:

Round Barn Winery operates year-round, though hours may vary by season:

- Spring & Summer (May–October): Open daily from 11 AM to 6 PM.
- Fall & Winter (November–April): Open daily from 12 PM to 5 PM. It is recommended to check their website or call ahead for event schedules and reservation availability during peak seasons.

Entry Fees:

There is no fee to enter the winery, but tastings and events have associated costs:

Your Digital Travel Companion
Scan to find recommended activities, digital guides, and beautiful images of this place.

Wineries & Breweries | 235 Cesar E. Chavez Ave SW, Grand Rapids, MI 49503

Founders Brewing Co.

Founders Brewing Co., located in downtown Grand Rapids, Michigan, is one of the most iconic craft breweries in the U.S. and a cornerstone of Grand Rapids' reputation as "Beer City, USA." Since its establishment in 1997, Founders has grown significantly and now occupies an entire city block. Known for its bold, flavorful beers like All Day IPA, Dirty Bastard, and the renowned KBS (Kentucky Breakfast Stout), Founders remains a must-visit destination for craft beer lovers.

Key Attractions:

- Taproom: The spacious taproom offers a laid-back atmosphere with a wide selection of beers, many of which are only available on-site. The venue includes both indoor seating and a popular outdoor beer garden. Founders also hosts regular live music, adding to the vibrant atmosphere.
- Tours: Founders offers brewery tours for those interested in learning about the brewing process. These tours, available on select days, cost $10 and include a Founders logo pint glass. They also offer a combined tour and tasting experience for $30, which includes exclusive beers.
- Kitchen: Founders revamped its kitchen in 2024 to offer a more diverse menu beyond its classic deli options. Dishes range from sandwiches to entrees like honey-glazed salmon, all designed to pair perfectly with their craft beers.

Best Time to Visit:

The taproom is open daily, with hours from 11 AM to 10 PM. For a more lively experience, visit during their happy hour (3 PM - 6 PM, Monday to Thursday), where pints are discounted. Summer months are perfect for enjoying the outdoor seating area, but the taproom stays busy year-round.

Entry Fees:

There is no entry fee to visit the taproom. However, brewery tours are available for a fee, with prices starting at $10 for a standard tour.

Your Digital Travel Companion
Scan to find recommended activities, digital guides, and beautiful images of this place.

Wineries & Breweries | 📍 716 S. Kalamazoo Street, Paw Paw, MI 49079

St. Julian Winery

St. Julian Winery, located in Paw Paw, Michigan, is the state's oldest and one of its most prestigious wineries. Established in 1921, this family-owned winery has been crafting award-winning wines, ciders, spirits, and juices for over a century. St. Julian offers a warm and inviting atmosphere where visitors can enjoy tastings, tours, and special events while learning about the rich history of Michigan winemaking. With a wide variety of wines to suit all palates, St. Julian is a must-visit destination for both novice and seasoned wine enthusiasts.

Key Attractions:

- Tasting Room: The spacious and welcoming tasting room at St. Julian Winery offers visitors a chance to sample a wide range of wines, from dry reds and whites to sweet wines and sparkling varieties. With knowledgeable staff on hand to guide you through the experience, you can taste and learn about the nuances of each wine.
- Wines & Beverages: St. Julian produces an extensive portfolio of wines and other beverages.
- Guided Tours: St. Julian offers guided tours of their winemaking facilities, giving visitors an insider's look at how their wines are produced, from the vineyard to the bottle. The tour includes an overview of their winemaking process, fermentation rooms, and barrel aging.

Best Time to Visit:

The best time to visit St. Julian Winery is during the spring and summer months

(May to October) when the vineyards are in bloom and outdoor events are in full swing.

Operating Hours:

St. Julian Winery operates year-round, with the following typical hours:

- Monday – Saturday: 10 AM – 6 PM
- Sunday: 12 PM – 6 PM It's always a good idea to check their website or call ahead for special event hours or holiday closures.

Entry Fees:

There is no fee to enter the winery, but tastings and tours come with associated costs:

Your Digital Travel Companion
Scan to find recommended activities, digital guides, and beautiful images of this place.

Family-Friendly Attractions

Notes

Family-Friendly Attractions |  1300 W. Fulton St., Grand Rapids, MI

John Ball Zoo

John Ball Zoo, located in Grand Rapids, Michigan, is a family-friendly destination that features over 2,000 animals from around the world. The zoo offers visitors the chance to explore diverse exhibits, including an aquarium, African savanna animals, and North and South American wildlife. Visitors can also enjoy interactive experiences like ziplining, a Sky Trail ropes course, and the funicular for sweeping views of the zoo and Grand Rapids.

Key Attractions:

- Animal Exhibits: Highlights include lions, tigers, chimpanzees, red pandas, and penguins. The zoo also features immersive environments like the African savanna and North American forests.
- Interactive Experiences: Try the four-story Sky Trail ropes course or take a thrilling ride on the 600-foot zipline. You can also pan for gems at the John Ball Zoo Gem Company or take the funicular for a relaxing ride around the zoo.

- Seasonal Events: Popular events include the Grand Rapids Lantern Festival and adult-only evenings where guests can enjoy cocktails.

Best Time to Visit:

John Ball Zoo operates from March 22 to November 24, with peak seasons during the summer. The fall offers cooler temperatures and fewer crowds, making it an excellent time to visit.

Operating Hours:

- Summer (May 25 – Sep. 2): Monday to Thursday: 9 AM - 6 PM; Friday to Sunday: 9 AM - 7 PM.
- Fall (Sep. 3 – Nov. 24): Open daily from 10 AM - 4 PM.

Entry Fees:

- Adults (13-61 years): $19.95 during fall (higher on weekends in summer at $24.95).
- Seniors (62+) and Youth (3-12 years): $14.95.
- Children (2 and under): Free.

Your Digital Travel Companion
Scan to find recommended activities, digital guides, and beautiful images of this place.

👪 Family-Friendly Attractions | 📍 7400 Division Dr., Battle Creek, MI 49014

Binder Park Zoo

Binder Park Zoo, located in Battle Creek, Michigan, is a 433-acre zoo that offers a unique mix of local and exotic wildlife exhibits, including the popular Wild Africa section. The zoo is a family-friendly destination with interactive experiences and engaging activities that cater to visitors of all ages.

Key Attractions:

- Wild Africa: A signature experience, accessible via the free Wilderness Tram, where guests can explore the savanna-like environment, see animals such as giraffes, zebras, and lions, and hand-feed giraffes at the Twiga Overlook.
- Z.O. & O. Railroad: A vintage 1963 miniature train that takes guests on a scenic 1.5-mile loop through the zoo ($3 per ride).
- Binda Conservation Carousel: A beautifully crafted carousel with hand-carved animals, perfect for all ages ($3 per ride).

- Zoo Dining: Beulah's Restaurant and Kalahari Kitchen offer a range of food options with views of the surrounding zoo.

Best Time to Visit:

Binder Park Zoo is open seasonally, typically from May 1 to October 27, making spring through fall the ideal time to visit. Hours vary slightly between weekdays and weekends:

- Weekdays (Mon-Fri): 9 AM to 5 PM
- Saturdays: 9 AM to 6 PM
- Sundays: 11 AM to 6 PM

Entry Fees:

- Adults: $17.75
- Seniors (65+): $16.25
- Children (2-10): $14.75
- Children (under 2): Free
- Parking: $3 per vehicle
- Military personnel receive a 50% discount, and AAA members get a 10% discount.

Your Digital Travel Companion
Scan to find recommended activities, digital guides, and beautiful images of this place.

Family-Friendly Attractions |  220 E. Ann St., Ann Arbor, MI 48104

Ann Arbor Hands-On Museum

The Ann Arbor Hands-On Museum, located in downtown Ann Arbor, Michigan, is an interactive science museum that sparks curiosity and learning for visitors of all ages. With over 250 exhibits across four floors, this museum focuses on science, technology, engineering, art, and math (STEAM) through engaging and hands-on activities.

Key Attractions:

- Interactive Exhibits: The museum features a variety of exhibits, including the H2Oh! Water Gallery, where kids can experiment with water, and the STEAM Park, filled with engineering and mechanical gadgets. Other popular exhibits include Light and Optics, All About You, and the 1930s Lyons' Country Store, where kids can play shopkeeper.
- Preschool Gallery: Designed for younger children (ages 0-4), this area allows them to explore water tables, dress up, and participate in imaginative play.

- Special Events: The museum regularly hosts special events, including wildlife encounters and seasonal holiday events, making each visit unique.

Best Time to Visit:

The museum is open year-round, but its hours are:

- Tuesday to Saturday: 10 AM – 5 PM
- Sunday: 12 PM – 5 PM
- Closed on Mondays.

Entry Fees:

- General Admission: $16 per person for adults and children.
- Children under 2: Free.
- Memberships: Family memberships are available for $100 annually, offering unlimited access for a year, which is a great deal for frequent visitors.

Your Digital Travel Companion
Scan to find recommended activities, digital guides, and beautiful images of this place.

👪 Family-Friendly Attractions | 📍 5401 Woodward Ave., Detroit, MI 48202

Detroit Historical Museum

The Detroit Historical Museum, located in Midtown Detroit, is dedicated to chronicling the rich history of Detroit and its role as an industrial powerhouse. It features a wide range of exhibits, including the Streets of Old Detroit, which recreates the city's streets from the 1840s through the early 20th century, and America's Motor City, which explores Detroit's significant role in the automobile industry. The museum also hosts exhibits on Detroit's brewing heritage and cultural contributions like music and sports.

Key Attractions:

- Streets of Old Detroit: Stroll through recreated streets showcasing what life was like in the 19th and early 20th centuries.
- Motor City Exhibit: Discover Detroit's automotive history, including how the city became synonymous with car manufacturing.
- Boom Town: Detroit in the 1920s: An exhibit highlighting Detroit's rapid growth and the contrasting social dynamics of the time.
- Detroit 67: Perspectives: A powerful exhibition exploring the events of July 1967 and their lasting impact on the city.

Best Time to Visit:

The museum is open year-round with the following hours:

- Wednesday – Saturday: 10 AM – 5 PM
- Sunday: 1 PM – 5 PM On the second Sunday of each month, admission is free, thanks to the Kresge Foundation.

Entry Fees:

- Adults: $10
- Seniors (60+), Students, Active Military, First Responders: $8
- Children (6-17): $6
- Children under 6: Free
- Household Pass (up to 6 people): $35 There is free admission for Detroit Historical Society members and Detroit residents.

Your Digital Travel Companion

Scan to find recommended activities, digital guides, and beautiful images of this place.

Family-Friendly Attractions | 4570 Huron River Pkwy, Milford, MI 48380

Kensington Metropark

Kensington Metropark, located in Milford, Michigan, is a vast natural retreat spanning over 4,481 acres, offering a wide variety of outdoor activities for visitors year-round. From its beautiful wooded trails and beaches to its farm and nature center, it provides endless opportunities for both recreation and relaxation.

Key Attractions:

- Beaches: Enjoy swimming and relaxing at Martindale Beach and Maple Beach, both equipped with accessible facilities and nearby playgrounds.
- Kensington Farm Center: A favorite among children, the farm center allows visitors to see and interact with farm animals like cows, pigs, and goats. It also hosts special events and educational workshops.
- Nature Trails: With nearly 12 miles of paved and unpaved trails, visitors can hike, bike, or simply enjoy the scenic views of Kent Lake and the surrounding landscapes.

- Boating & Fishing: Rent a canoe or kayak to explore Kent Lake, or take advantage of fishing opportunities at designated spots.
- Winter Activities: During winter months, Kensington Metropark offers cross-country skiing, snowshoeing, and tobogganing.
- Golf & Disc Golf: The park features an 18-hole golf course and a disc golf course, making it a perfect destination for sports enthusiasts.

Best Time to Visit:

Kensington Metropark is open year-round, from 6 AM to 10 PM daily. Whether you're looking to enjoy a summer day at the beach or explore the snowy trails in winter, there's always something to do.

Entry Fees:

- Daily Vehicle Pass: $10
- Annual Metroparks Pass: $40, which grants access to all Huron-Clinton Metroparks.

Your Digital Travel Companion
Scan to find recommended activities, digital guides, and beautiful images of this place.

Family-Friendly Attractions |  5020 John R St., Detroit, MI 48202

Michigan Science Center

The Michigan Science Center (MiSci), located in Midtown Detroit, is a dynamic hands-on museum that focuses on engaging visitors of all ages in the fields of science, technology, engineering, and math (STEM). With over 220 interactive exhibits, live stage shows, and multiple theaters, it provides an immersive and educational experience for families, school groups, and curious individuals.

Key Attractions:

- IMAX Dome Theater: One of the largest screens in Michigan, the IMAX Dome provides stunning, immersive films on topics like space, nature, and science.
- Planetarium: Experience the night sky and explore the universe through engaging shows like One World, One Sky featuring Big Bird and Elmo.
- Toyota 4D Engineering Theater: Combining 3D visuals with physical effects, this theater delivers a multi-sensory experience, with shows like Volcanoes: The Fires of Creation.

- Hands-On Exhibits: From physics demonstrations to health and biology exhibits, the center offers a wide array of interactive activities.

Best Time to Visit:

The Michigan Science Center is open from Tuesday to Sunday, 10 AM to 4 PM, and is closed on Mondays. Special events and theater shows occur throughout the year, so it's worth checking their schedule for specific exhibitions or educational programs.

Entry Fees:

- $23 per person for ages 3 and up

Your Digital Travel Companion
Scan to find recommended activities, digital guides, and beautiful images of this place.

👪 Family-Friendly Attractions | 📍 39221 Woodward Ave, Bloomfield Hills, MI 48303-0801 ✈

Cranbrook Institute of Science

Cranbrook Institute of Science, located in Bloomfield Hills, Michigan, is a natural history and science museum offering visitors a wide range of exhibits and interactive experiences. Known for its engaging displays on geology, anthropology, astronomy, and more, the museum is a great destination for families and science enthusiasts.

Key Attractions:

- Acheson Planetarium: Enjoy immersive astronomy shows in this popular planetarium, with tickets priced at $5 for adults and children alike.
- Permanent Exhibits: Highlights include a full-size Tyrannosaurus rex skeleton cast, the Mineral Study Gallery with over 1,800 specimens, and hands-on exhibits exploring natural history, fossils, and geology.
- Cranbrook Observatory: Open to the public on select days for stargazing and solar observation, this facility offers a fantastic experience for astronomy fans.

Best Time to Visit:

The museum is open year-round, but hours vary:

- Wednesday to Thursday: 10 AM - 5 PM
- Friday: 10 AM - 10 PM (with special $5 admission after 5 PM)
- Saturday: 10 AM - 5 PM
- Sunday: 12 PM - 4 PM The first Friday of each month offers free admission from 5 PM to 9 PM, courtesy of the MASCO Corporation Foundation.

Entry Fees:

- Adults: $14
- Children (2-12 years): $10.50
- Seniors (65+): $10.50
- Children under 2: Free
- Discounts and free admission are available for certain events, such as the "Free First Friday".

Your Digital Travel Companion
Scan to find recommended activities, digital guides, and beautiful images of this place.

Family-Friendly Attractions | ◉ 4316 Baldwin Rd, Auburn Hills, MI 48326

SEA LIFE Michigan Aquarium

SEA LIFE Michigan Aquarium, located at Great Lakes Crossing Outlets in Auburn Hills, is the largest aquarium in the state, featuring over 250 species and more than 2,000 individual creatures. Visitors can explore a variety of exhibits, including sharks, rays, sea turtles, and the interactive Touchpool, where you can touch marine life like sea stars and anemones. It's an excellent family-friendly destination that provides both educational and immersive experiences.

Key Attractions:

- Interactive Touchpool: Get hands-on with marine life such as crabs and sea stars.
- Ocean Tunnel: Walk through a 180-degree ocean tunnel and come face-to-face with sharks and other sea creatures swimming around you.
- Stingray Bay: A unique exhibit where visitors can view and learn more about different species of stingrays.
- Conservation Talks: Educational presentations about marine

conservation and animal care, enhancing your visit with valuable insights into aquatic life.

Best Time to Visit:

The aquarium is open daily:

- Monday to Saturday: 10 AM to 7 PM
- Sunday: 11 AM to 6 PM It's recommended to visit during weekdays or early mornings to avoid crowds, especially during school holidays or weekends.

Entry Fees:

- Adults (13+): $24.99 (when purchased on-site) or $19.99 if you book online in advance.
- Children (3-12): $19.99 at the door.
- Children under 3: Free There are also combo tickets available that include entry to LEGOLAND Discovery Center, starting at $27.99 per person when purchased online

Your Digital Travel Companion
Scan to find recommended activities, digital guides, and beautiful images of this place.

Family-Friendly Attractions | 📍 4240 Baldwin Rd, Auburn Hills, MI 48326

LEGOLAND Discovery Center Michigan

LEGOLAND Discovery Center Michigan, located in Auburn Hills, is the ultimate indoor LEGO playground, specifically designed for families with children aged 3 to 10. With a variety of creative and interactive attractions, this destination offers endless fun and learning opportunities for kids and families alike.

Key Attractions:

- MINILAND: Explore miniature versions of Detroit-area landmarks built with over 1.5 million LEGO bricks.
- Kingdom Quest Ride: Hop aboard a chariot to rescue the captured princess in this interactive LEGO ride.
- Merlin's Apprentice Ride: Pedal your way to help Merlin cast his magical spells.
- LEGO 4D Cinema: Watch your favorite LEGO characters come to life in an immersive 4D experience with wind, rain, and lighting effects.

Best Time to Visit:

LEGOLAND Discovery Center is open daily from 10 AM to 6 PM, with the last entry at 4:30 PM. Visiting on weekdays or after 2 PM is recommended for a less crowded experience.

Entry Fees:

- Online Saver Ticket: From $19.99 per person.
- Walk-Up Admission: $24.99 per person.
- Children under 2: Free. Combo tickets with SEA LIFE Aquarium are available starting from $44.99, offering access to both attractions.

Your Digital Travel Companion
Scan to find recommended activities, digital guides, and beautiful images of this place.

👫 Family-Friendly Attractions | 📍 1602 W University Ave, Flint, MI 48504

Flint Children's Museum

The Flint Children's Museum is an interactive, hands-on museum located on the campus of Kettering University in Flint, Michigan. Designed for children aged 0-10, the museum offers over 40 fun and educational exhibits that encourage creative play and learning through exploration.

Key Attractions:

- Our Town: This imaginative play area allows children to step into roles like a veterinarian, firefighter, or shopkeeper in a miniature town, fostering creativity and role-playing.
- How Things Work: Kids can experiment with physics concepts in this exhibit through hands-on activities like an augmented reality sandbox.
- Sproutside: An outdoor space offering messy art projects and educational activities that emphasize physical activity and environmental learning.

Best Time to Visit:

The museum is open year-round with the following hours:

- Tuesday to Saturday: 10 AM – 4 PM
- Sunday: 12 PM – 4 PM On the second Sunday of each month, the museum hosts Sensory Sundays from 10 AM to 12 PM, offering a quieter environment tailored to children with sensory processing needs.

Entry Fees:

- General Admission: $8 per person (adults and children).
- Special Programs: Families with an EBT or WIC card can gain free admission for up to four people.

Your Digital Travel Companion
Scan to find recommended activities, digital guides, and beautiful images of this place.

Educational & Museums

Notes

🏛 Educational & Museums | 📍 1105 North University Avenue, Ann Arbor, MI 48109

University of Michigan Museum of Natural History

The University of Michigan Museum of Natural History in Ann Arbor offers a fascinating exploration of the natural world, with exhibits covering everything from dinosaurs to molecular biology. Located in the Biological Sciences Building, the museum blends engaging interactive exhibits with cutting-edge scientific research.

Key Attractions:

- Dinosaur Exhibits: Visitors can see reconstructed skeletons of prehistoric creatures, including mastodons and other iconic fossils.
- Planetarium & Dome Theater: The museum's state-of-the-art planetarium offers shows that explore the universe, taking viewers beyond the stars and deep into the ocean. Shows like "Sky Tonight" and "Tales of the Maya Skies" provide a fantastic immersive experience

- Exploring Michigan: Learn about the ecosystems of Michigan and how they've shaped the natural history of the region.
- Interactive Labs: Touch real specimens and use high-tech tools in the museum's interactive learning spaces, bringing science to life for all ages.

Best Time to Visit:

- September – May: Open Tuesday to Sunday from 10 AM to 4 PM.
- June – August: Open daily from 10 AM to 5 PM. The museum is closed on major holidays.

Entry Fees:

- General Admission: Free for individuals and families, although donations are appreciated. Tickets for planetarium shows cost $8 per person. Tickets for planetarium shows cost $5 per person for 45 minute programs.

Your Digital Travel Companion

Scan to find recommended activities, digital guides, and beautiful images of this place.

Educational & Museums | 315 E Warren Ave, Detroit, MI 48201

Charles H. Wright Museum of African American History

The Charles H. Wright Museum of African American History, located in Detroit, Michigan, is one of the largest institutions dedicated to preserving African American history and culture. The museum offers over 35,000 artifacts and multiple exhibitions that explore the struggles, triumphs, and contributions of African Americans from Africa through the modern era. One of the museum's most famous exhibits, "And Still We Rise", takes visitors through the history of African Americans, from the African continent to the Civil Rights Movement in the United States.

Key Attractions:

- 'And Still We Rise' Exhibit: This powerful permanent exhibit spans African American history and culture, from ancient African civilizations through the horrors of slavery and into modern-day achievements and civil rights movements.

- Tuskegee Airmen Exhibit: A hands-on, interactive experience highlighting the history and achievements of the legendary Tuskegee Airmen, perfect for aviation enthusiasts.

Best Time to Visit:

The museum is open:

- Thursday – Saturday: 9 AM – 4 PM
- Sunday: 12 PM – 5 PM The museum is closed on Mondays through Wednesdays.

Entry Fees:

- Adults (ages 18-61): $15
- Seniors (ages 62 and over): $12
- Youth (ages 6-17): $12
- Children (ages 0-5): Free
- Museum Members: Free

Your Digital Travel Companion

Scan to find recommended activities, digital guides, and beautiful images of this place.

🏛 Educational & Museums | 📍 272 Pearl St NW, Grand Rapids, MI 49504

Grand Rapids Public Museum

The Grand Rapids Public Museum, located in downtown Grand Rapids, Michigan, is a family-friendly destination that offers a deep dive into the natural, cultural, and scientific history of West Michigan and beyond. The museum features three floors of interactive exhibits, a planetarium, and even a historic carousel (though currently under renovation). It's an ideal destination for families, students, and curious minds of all ages.

Key Attractions:

- Streets of Old Grand Rapids: Step back in time to explore a recreated 1890s street scene, complete with storefronts and historical settings.
- Roger B. Chaffee Planetarium: Offering engaging shows on space, the planetarium is perfect for stargazing and learning about astronomy.
- Finny the Whale: A 76-foot-long finback whale skeleton that has been part of the museum since 1905,

offering a majestic insight into the natural world.
- Fashion + Nature Exhibit: An exhibit that explores the relationship between fashion and the environment.

Best Time to Visit:

- Monday to Friday: 9 AM – 5 PM
- Saturday and Sunday: 10 AM – 5 PM.

Entry Fees:

- Adults (18-61): $12
- Seniors (62+): $10
- Children (3-17) and Students with ID: $5
- Children under 3: Free Additional fees apply for planetarium shows ($4 with admission, $5 without), and special exhibits may also require extra fees.

Your Digital Travel Companion
Scan to find recommended activities, digital guides, and beautiful images of this place.

Educational & Museums |  39221 Woodward Ave, Bloomfield Hills, MI 48303

Cranbrook Art Museum

Best Time to Visit:

- Wednesday to Sunday: 11 AM – 5 PM.
- Thursdays: Extended hours until 8 PM, with free admission after 5 PM.

Entry Fees:

- General Admission: $10
- Seniors (65+): $8
- Students (with ID): $6
- Children 12 and under: Free
- Detroit residents: $8.

The Cranbrook Art Museum, located in Bloomfield Hills, Michigan, is a renowned cultural institution showcasing modern and contemporary art, architecture, and design. It is part of the larger Cranbrook Educational Community and features a wide range of rotating exhibitions, programs, and activities for art lovers.

Key Attractions:

- Current Exhibitions: The museum hosts rotating exhibitions focusing on the achievements of 20th and 21st-century artists, particularly those associated with the Cranbrook Academy of Art.
- Saarinen House: Visitors can explore this historic Art Deco home on the Cranbrook campus, designed by renowned architect Eliel Saarinen.
- Sculpture Garden: Wander through beautiful outdoor spaces filled with sculptures that complement the museum's architecture.

Your Digital Travel Companion

Scan to find recommended activities, digital guides, and beautiful images of this place.

🏛 Educational & Museums | 📍 314 S. Park Street, Kalamazoo, MI 49007

Kalamazoo Institute of Arts

The Kalamazoo Institute of Arts (KIA), located in downtown Kalamazoo, Michigan, is a vibrant cultural institution that focuses on visual arts, offering a rich collection of over 4,700 pieces, with a special emphasis on American art. The museum also features rotating special exhibits, which highlight both local and international artists. In addition to its exhibits, KIA provides art education through its Kirk Newman Art School, offering classes and workshops for all ages.

Key Attractions:

- Permanent Collection: The museum houses works from American artists across various media, including paintings, sculptures, and decorative arts.
- Special Exhibitions: KIA regularly rotates special exhibitions, showcasing diverse artistic styles and historical periods. Past exhibitions have included works by Dale Chihuly and thematic art collections.

- Kirk Newman Art School: The museum's art school offers art-making opportunities and workshops for both beginners and advanced artists.

Best Time to Visit:

The museum is open:

- Wednesday to Saturday: 11 AM to 5 PM
- Sunday: 12 PM to 4 PM On the fourth Thursday of each month, the museum extends its hours until 8 PM, with free admission from 5 PM to 8 PM.

Entry Fees:

- Adults: $10
- Seniors (60+): $8
- Students (18+ with ID): $7
- Youth (7-17): $5
- Children under 6: Free The museum offers discounts for active-duty military personnel and through special programs like "Museums for All," which provides reduced admission for EBT cardholders.

Your Digital Travel Companion

Scan to find recommended activities, digital guides, and beautiful images of this place.

Educational & Museums | 📍 18335 N Whitefish Point Rd, Paradise, MI 49768

Great Lakes Shipwreck Museum

Located at Whitefish Point in Michigan's Upper Peninsula, the Great Lakes Shipwreck Museum is a must-visit destination for those interested in maritime history. This museum focuses on the dramatic shipwrecks of Lake Superior, including the famous SS Edmund Fitzgerald. Visitors can learn about over 200 shipwrecks, explore historical structures, and discover the human stories behind these tragedies.

Key Attractions:

- Main Gallery: Featuring artifacts from 13 shipwrecks, including the original bell from the SS Edmund Fitzgerald, this exhibit highlights the powerful history of Lake Superior's shipwrecks.
- Whitefish Point Light Station: Explore Michigan's oldest active lighthouse, which has been guiding ships since 1861. Visitors can tour the lightkeeper's quarters to see how lighthouse families lived.
- Historical Structures: Additional sites include the 1923 Lifeboat Station

Surfboat House and the 1920s U.S. Navy Radio Building, both of which are key parts of the museum's historical narrative.

Best Time to Visit:

The museum is open May 1 to October 31, from 10 AM to 6 PM daily. The last full-price ticket is sold at 5 PM.

Entry Fees:

- Adults: $15
- Children (6-17): $11
- Children (under 5): Free
- Family Pass (2 adults and 2+ children): $50.

Your Digital Travel Companion
Scan to find recommended activities, digital guides, and beautiful images of this place.

🏛 Educational & Museums | 📍 296 W Webster Ave, Muskegon, MI 49440

Muskegon Museum of Art

The Muskegon Museum of Art (MMA), located in Muskegon, Michigan, is a cultural gem offering an impressive collection of fine art, featuring American and European artists. Known for works by artists such as Edward Hopper, Camille Pissarro, and Dale Chihuly, the museum regularly hosts a variety of exhibitions and public programs.

Key Attractions:

- Permanent Collection: The museum boasts a range of paintings, sculptures, and decorative arts from American and European artists.
- Special Exhibits: Throughout the year, the museum features temporary exhibitions such as the 95th Michigan Contemporary Art Exhibition, showcasing local talent and innovation.
- Sculpture Garden: Visitors can also explore outdoor sculptures in the museum's surrounding areas, adding an extra layer of art exploration.

Best Time to Visit:

- Tuesday, Wednesday, Friday, Saturday, Sunday: 11 AM – 5 PM
- Thursday: 11 AM – 8 PM (Free admission after 5 PM)
- Closed on Mondays and major holidays.

Entry Fees:

- Adults: $12
- Seniors (65+): $8
- Students (17+ with ID): $6
- Children (16 and under): Free Free admission is offered on the second Saturday of each month, thanks to support from Howmet Aerospace.

Your Digital Travel Companion
Scan to find recommended activities, digital guides, and beautiful images of this place.

Ready to Capture Your Michigan Memories?

Your Travel Journal

Welcome to your personal Michigan adventure journal! This is your space to record the moments, memories, and discoveries that make each destination unforgettable. Whether it's a scenic view, a hidden gem, or a favorite local spot, let this journal capture the spirit of your journey. So, grab your pen and get ready to create a keepsake of your Michigan travels!

Travel Journal – Michigan

Date:	Weather:	Location	Rating

First Impressions

Memorable Moments

What Made This Place Special?

Would I come back again?

☐ YES   ☐ NO

A New Discovery I have made

Travel Journal – Michigan

Date:	Weather:	Location	Rating
	☀ ⛅ ☁ 🌧 ⛈ 🌨		☆☆☆☆☆

First Impressions

Memorable Moments

What Made This Place Special?

Would I come back again?

☐ YES   ☐ NO

A New Discovery I have made

Travel Journal – Michigan

Date:	Weather:	Location	Rating
	☀ ⛅ ☁ 🌧 ⛈ 🌨		☆☆☆☆☆

First Impressions

Memorable Moments

What Made This Place Special?

Would I come back again?

☐ YES   ☐ NO

A New Discovery I have made

Travel Journal – Michigan

Date:	Weather:	Location	Rating
	☀ ⛅ ☁ 🌧 ⛈ 🌨		☆☆☆☆☆

First Impressions

Memorable Moments

What Made This Place Special?

Would I come back again?

☐ YES   ☐ NO

A New Discovery I have made

Travel Journal – Michigan

Date:	Weather:	Location	Rating
	☀ ⛅ ☁ 🌧 ⛈ 🌨		☆☆☆☆☆

First Impressions

Memorable Moments

What Made This Place Special?

Would I come back again?

☐ YES ☐ NO

A New Discovery I have made

Travel Journal – Michigan

Date:	Weather:	Location	Rating
	☀ ⛅ ☁ 🌧 ⛈ 🌨		☆☆☆☆☆

First Impressions

Memorable Moments

What Made This Place Special?

Would I come back again?

☐ YES   ☐ NO

A New Discovery I have made

Travel Journal – Michigan

Date:	Weather:	Location	Rating
	☀ ⛅ ☁ 🌧 ⛈ 🌨		☆☆☆☆☆

First Impressions

Memorable Moments

What Made This Place Special?

Would I come back again?

☐ YES   ☐ NO

A New Discovery I have made

Travel Journal – Michigan

Date:	Weather:	Location	Rating
	☀ ⛅ ☁ 🌧 ⛈ 🌨		☆☆☆☆☆

First Impressions

Memorable Moments

What Made This Place Special?

Would I come back again?

☐ YES   ☐ NO

A New Discovery I have made

Travel Journal – Michigan

Date:	Weather:	Location	Rating
	☀ ⛅ ☁ 🌧 ⛈ 🌨		☆☆☆☆☆

First Impressions

Memorable Moments

What Made This Place Special?

Would I come back again?

☐ YES   ☐ NO

A New Discovery I have made

Travel Journal – Michigan

Date:	Weather:	Location	Rating
	☀ ⛅ ☁ 🌧 ⛈ 🌨		☆☆☆☆☆

First Impressions

Memorable Moments

What Made This Place Special?

Would I come back again?

☐ YES   ☐ NO

A New Discovery I have made

Thank You for Exploring Michigan with Us!

As we reach the end of this guide, we want to extend our heartfelt thanks. We're thrilled that you chose LocalListingX as your companion on this journey through Michigan's wonders. It's been a privilege to be part of your adventures, and we hope these pages have inspired lasting memories.

We're always working to make this book even better, and your feedback plays a crucial role in helping us do so. By sharing your experience, you not only help us improve but also guide future travelers in discovering Michigan's beauty.

If you encounter any issues or have questions, please don't hesitate to contact us at info@infiniteinkpress.org. We're here to help and ensure you have the best possible experience.

How to Leave a Review

If you have a moment, we'd be grateful if you could leave a review on Amazon. Simply scan the QR code below, which will take you directly to the review page. Your thoughts, favorite spots, and insights mean a lot to us—and to the readers who will follow in your footsteps.

Thank you once again for choosing LocalListingX. We hope this book has sparked a deeper love for Michigan and its many treasures. Safe travels, and may your future journeys be filled with discovery!

Warm regards,
The LocalListingX Team

Conclusion

Michigan is a state of contrasts and surprises, where rugged coastlines meet serene inland lakes, and bustling cities coexist with tranquil forests. As you've journeyed through the pages of this book, you've encountered over 100 unique destinations, each offering a glimpse into what makes Michigan such a compelling place to explore. From the quiet beauty of the Great Lakes to the cultural vibrancy of historic towns and cities, Michigan invites you to discover its diverse landscapes, rich traditions, and welcoming communities.

Every destination on this bucket list has its own story, a story that adds to the rich tapestry of Michigan's identity. Whether you were drawn to the pristine shores of Lake Michigan, the rolling dunes of the national lakeshore, or the fascinating history of places like Mackinac Island, each location offers a window into a different aspect of the state's heritage and character. This journey has highlighted Michigan's remarkable blend of natural beauty, innovation, and deep-rooted traditions, capturing the spirit of the Great Lakes State in all its variety.

But Michigan is more than a collection of destinations; it's a place that invites connection and introspection. As you check off each experience on this bucket list, remember that this state offers more than just scenic views and historical sites. It provides moments of peace and reflection, whether you're watching the sun set over Lake Superior, wandering through a quiet forest trail, or tasting the flavors of Michigan's local produce at a bustling farmer's market. Each experience contributes to a journey of discovery, connection, and joy that will stay with you long after you leave.

Michigan's charm lies in its ability to blend the familiar with the extraordinary. You can hike through ancient forests, wander along endless shorelines, or experience the energy of a festival that has been celebrated for generations. And each time you return, you'll find something new waiting for you—a hidden waterfall, a vibrant local art scene, or a quiet lakeside town filled with charm. The state's beauty is timeless, yet it continues to evolve, offering fresh discoveries with every season.

As you explore, remember that Michigan is a place where adventure meets tranquility, where you can find both thrill and peace. It's a state that rewards those who seek to know it deeply, from its vibrant urban centers to its untouched natural reserves. Embrace the journey, keep an open heart, and allow Michigan to surprise you with its boundless landscapes and enduring spirit.

So whether this is your first journey through Michigan or a return to familiar places, let this guide be just the beginning. There will always be more to uncover, more paths to wander, and more memories to make in this remarkable state. Michigan is a place that beckons you to return, time and again, to rediscover its wonders and write new stories. Here's to your adventures yet to come and to the countless memories waiting to be made in the heart of the Great Lakes State.